Pillars in Ethiopian History

HANSBERRY, William Leo. Pillars in Ethiopian history; the William Leo Hansberry African history notebook. v.1, ed. by Joseph E. Harris. Howard University, 1974. 154p map bibl 73-88970. 8.95. ISBN 0-88258-009-4. C.I.P.

CHOICE   APR. '75

History, Geography &
Travel

Africa

DT 381
H24

This book is more than a collection of four essays dealing with ancient and medieval Ethiopian history and posthumously drawn from unpublished manuscripts, for Hansberry has long been acclaimed as one of the unsung leading black scholars of the first half of this century. Although he published very little in his lifetime, Hansberry's notebooks indicate considerable scholarly expertise in handling such difficult materials as the role of the Queen of Sheba legend in Ethiopian history, the establishment of Christianity as the state religion 16 centuries ago, the Prester John legend, and the subsequent contacts between Ethiopia and Europe in the 15th century. The editor's introduction gives a good, but occasionally apologetic biography of Hansberry. Unfortunately, the editor did little more than transcribe Hansberry's notebooks and consequently failed to put Hansberry's work in scholarly perspective. Nevertheless, the book is important, perhaps more for black studies than for African studies, because it gives Hansberry the broader general audience he so richly deserves as a pioneer Africanist.

SSINS

SABEE

o Ebba

NEGRANA
Najran

PUDNU
KINANA KINDAY
KINAIDOKOLPITES

Sa'ada o

El Djauf

I Farasa

SABA

o MARI

RASID

o Lohera

N'aad

o Sanaa

HAMDANITES

Hamdan (A) 2400 ~

HIMYARITES

SEBID

I Dahlac
I ORINE

HOMERITES

DULES

BERENICE PANCHRUSOS
MAXIMUM EMPORIUM TROGLODITORUM

DAFAR
HAVALAN

o Bagil

Hq deida

GEEZ

DamarDAN o

o SAFAR TAPH

PAI

ANTIPHILI PORTUS

Yerim

D

to

ANNINE
METINE

O

Edil o

AFARS ou DANAKES

HABISA

MOUSA Musa o

AGALMAN

Dhala

TANNA

KATABA

KATABA
o

MO
MO
alle
DERTA
to

Taie

NGABENES
ANGOT

ATHAGAOUS (?)

THOMMA (Time)

AGUEZAT

o Moka

Lahadj

AZab o

TSIDIS INS

KATABANES

(Saba)

o AD

W Ala

FL Anazo

GALLA

ADELS

W Haouacbe

ANIE

COLONIE FRANÇAISE

OCE LIS

DIODORI INSULA . Perim

ARSINOE ?

Oboek o

DIRE PROM.

Baie de Tadjoura

RAUSOI TROGLODITICA

Djibouti

SAULATE

AUALITES EMP

Zeila

Magdala

Fer d'Addis Abbaba

Grandes majusc
Petites majuscul
Minuscules
Minuscules soul
Majuscules soul

BOOKS BY JOSEPH E. HARRIS

Africans and Their History

*The African Presence in Asia: Consequences of the
East African Slave Trade*

About the Editor

Joseph Harris, a graduate of Howard University
and a student of William Hansberry, has been an
African history instructor at Williams College
(Massachusetts), an associate professor of African
history at State University College (New Paltz,
New York), and is currently a professor in the
Department of History, University of Nairobi,
Kenya. Professor Harris has also lectured on the
CBS "Black Heritage" series and written two books:
Consequences of the East African Slave Trade
(Northwestern University Press) and *Africans and
Their History* (New American Library).

Pillars in Ethiopian History

The William Leo Hansberry African History Notebook

VOLUME I

Edited by Joseph E. Harris

HOWARD UNIVERSITY PRESS
WASHINGTON, D.C.
1974

Printed in the United States of America

Endpaper map courtesy of Geography Map Division, Library of Congress. Jim Wells, photographer.

Library of Congress Cataloging in Publication Data

Hansberry, William Leo.
   Pillars in Ethiopian history.

   1. Ethiopia—History—Addresses, essays, lectures.
   2. Ethiopia—Historiography—Addresses, essays, lectures.
   I. Title.
   DT381.H35   963'.007'2   73-88970
   ISBN 0-88258-009-4

To the memory of William Leo Hansberry and to his wife, Myrtle Kelso Hansberry

Preface

Although William Leo Hansberry's works are over a generation late in appearing, this book is still valuable to the general reader, for whom it is primarily intended, and to many specialists. Unfortunately, Professor Hansberry was unable to complete this work during his lifetime. I therefore consider it appropriate and necessary to include a chapter on the man himself. While the chapter cannot do full justice to him or his career, it should help readers to understand the man, his ideas, ideals, and aspirations during the time in which he lived. This is especially important because of the nature of his career as a pioneer Africanist whose full influence never surfaced, primarily because he predated his times with innovative ideas about African history and its place in education, particularly as that education related to Africans and Afro-Americans.

For over fifty years Hansberry collected various kinds of data on African history and accumulated an impressive personal collection of notes, lectures, speeches, books, articles, pamphlets, and visual aids pertaining to the whole field of African studies. This collection is known as the Hansberry Private Papers (HPP), and is in the possession of his wife, Myrtle Kelso Hansberry. There is a smaller collection, known as the Hansberry File, in the Moorland-Spingarn Collection at Howard University. Although much of the second collection is contained in fuller form in the first, both are significant and comprise the major source of written materials by and about William Leo Hansberry.

This volume has been drawn from only a small portion of Hansberry's materials; much remains for future research. I should point out, however, that many of the materials I have used are in lecture form, prepared for classroom use by Hansberry himself. I therefore encountered the problem of trying to assemble and relate papers I thought would reflect Professor Hansberry's thinking. This risky task resulted in the four essays included in this book; but I emphasize that Hansberry wrote them as narrative history and not as essays. However, since some of them were incomplete (whether because Hansberry did not finish them or because they have been lost, or due to the unavailability of data), and since many of the subjects he covered have been written about in recent years by several scholars and general writers, I decided to select a central theme around which a few pieces could be organized as essays. This seemed not only a stimulating approach but also one which would reveal the continued relevance of Hansberry's work. Fortunately, he focused much of his scholarly efforts on ancient and medieval Ethiopian history, so the essays in this volume very conveniently deal with what I regard as vital traditional pillars of Ethiopian history. These pillars—the Queen of Sheba legend, the origin and development of Ethiopian Christianity, and medieval international relations—support the book's central theme, namely, the basic roots of Ethiopian unity.

While I chose the theme and selected the individual essays, the content and style remain Professor Hansberry's, with the exception of the introductory comments preceding each chapter, and the explanatory footnotes dispersed throughout. I decided to keep the footnotes at a minimum for two basic reasons: first, Hansberry seldom used them, no doubt assuming, as other authorities have, that years of training and experience qualify one for reaching individual conclusions without extensive documentation; and I wanted to present the materials as nearly as possible as Hansberry would have done. This should indeed facilitate a more authentic evaluation of his work. Second, the book is intended for general readership, as I believe he would have preferred.

The term notebook seemed an appropriate title to me because most of the materials for the book's substance appeared in note and lecture form for classroom use. Moreover, Hansberry is often regarded as essentially a teacher who also supplied Africana information to anyone who wanted it. So, I have chosen the general label, The William Leo Hansberry African History Notebook, for this and any subsequent volume I may edit.

The reader is reminded that the Hansberry Private Papers (HPP) are not limited only to notes and lectures. There is an extensive file of letters; two large and well-organized scrapbooks contain valuable personal and professional information; there are many pamphlets, newspaper clippings, reports, minutes of meetings, announcements, graphs, photographs, slides, commendations, and rare books.

The history behind the publication of Hansberry's work is long and complex but I emphasize here that the whole idea may have foundered had it not been for the dedicated and determined efforts of Professor Hansberry's wife, Myrtle Kelso. Since their marriage in 1937, she has been the most avid supporter of her husband's ideas and goals. A trained linguist, she not only gave Hansberry inspiration and strength to endure the difficult life of a pioneer academic with unpopular ideas, she also served as his research assistant, translator, and typist. For several years after Hansberry's death, she and her family continued to assemble, document, and type many of his unfinished papers. Indeed, in 1971 after I assumed editorial responsibilities for the papers I received fully cooperative and valuable assistance from the Hansberrys; and I am most grateful for that.

I also take this opportunity to acknowledge the keen interest and support provided by Charles F. Harris, first as Senior Editor at Random House and later as Executive Director of the Howard University Press. Random House's interest, initiated by Hansberry, declined and soon disappeared when Charles Harris resigned as Senior Editor. However, the commitment to publication of this work became a central concern of the Howard University Press, and it is largely due to the Executive Director's efforts that this volume has appeared and others are projected.

I extend thanks to Professor Ephraim Issac of Harvard University for reading and commenting on a portion of the manuscript. I also express thanks to the staff of Stetson Library at Williams College for the kind assistance I received from them.

Although Howard University did not accord Professor Hansberry the honor he deserved during his lifetime, it is especially fitting that his first volume appear under the auspices of the Howard University Press.

February 1974

Joseph E. Harris
Department of History
Williams College
Williamstown, Massachusetts

Contents

Pillars in Ethiopian History

William Leo Hansberry, 1894-1965
Profile of a Pioneer Africanist

Along with W. E. B. Du Bois and Carter G. Woodson, Hansberry probably did more than any other scholar in these early days to advance the study of the culture and civilization of Africa.

Williston H. Lofton
Howard University

You [Hansberry] initiated me into the sanctuaries of anthropology and ancient African history.

Letter from Nnamdi Azikiwe
First President of Nigeria

Mr. Hansberry, a professor at Howard University, is the one modern scholar who has tried to study the Negro in Egypt and Ethiopia.

Foreword, The World and Africa
W. E. B. Du Bois

Williston Lofton, one of Hansberry's students, was later a colleague and office mate at Howard University; Nnamdi Azikiwe was also Hansberry's student and a friend. William E. B. Du Bois was Hansberry's mentor. His scholarship in-

3

spired Hansberry as early as 1916. These three have captured the central theme of Hansberry's professional career: he was a pioneer whose influence spread from the diaspora to Africa and impressed both blacks and whites.*

This great achievement had its beginning in Gloster, Mississippi, where Hansberry was born. At the death of his father, a professor at Alcorn A. & M. College in Mississippi, the family inherited "a reasonably well-stocked library" with many books on ancient history. This no doubt influenced young Hansberry and became his first guidepost along the way to his future career. In the son's own words: "I acquired, while still quite young, a deep interest in the stirring epic of human strivings in the distant and romantic ages . . . and by the end of my freshman year in college at old Atlanta University I had become, largely through independent reading . . . something of an authority on the 'glory that was Greece' and the 'grandeur that was Rome.'" But he was unable in his search to add to his "exceedingly limited knowledge of Black Africa's story in olden days." Although he did not then comprehend the fact of, and reasons for, the distortion and suppression of African and Afro-American history, he was "tempted" to question the general theory that prior to European discovery in the fifteenth century "Black Africa was

---

* Symbolic of Professor Hansberry within the context of the Pan African tradition is the following: When Hansberry died, Edward W. Blyden III was Director of the Hansberry Institute of African Studies located in the Russwurm Building at the University of Nigeria in Nsukka which was established largely because of the efforts of Nnamdi Azikiwe. For those who wish a fuller understanding of the import of this, consult: Hollis Lynch, *Edward Wilmot Blyden* (London, 1967); the several works by Blyden himself; Robert W. July, *The Origins of Modern African Thought* (New York, 1967); Jean H. Kopytoff, *A Preface to Modern Nigeria* (Madison, Wisc., 1965); and Joseph E. Harris, "The Unveiling of a Pioneer," *A Tribute to the Memory of Professor William Leo Hansberry* (Department of History, Howard, 1972).

altogether devoid of any history worthy of serious academic concern."

During the summer of 1916, a second guidepost appeared when Hansberry read W. E. B. Du Bois's book, *The Negro*, which included chapters on kingdoms and empires in tropical Africa during ancient and medieval times. These revelations took Hansberry by surprise. For the first time he read about the various societies and kingdoms in ancient and medieval Africa. Hansberry was thus inspired to pursue the subject further by reading several of the books cited in Du Bois's "Suggestions For Further Reading." Unable to obtain the books he wanted at Atlanta University, Hansberry transferred to Harvard College where he pursued courses relating to Africa in anthropology and archaeology. He received his B.A. degree in 1921 and the M.A. degree in 1932, both at Harvard.

The Harvard experience better prepared Hansberry to pursue his mission in African studies. He became deeply concerned over the lack of efforts by black schools and colleges to make use of recent discoveries and studies which confirmed that Africans and their descendants have an honorable, and indeed glorious, past. The time had arrived, in his view, for blacks to affirm their identity by displaying a self-confidence which only a true knowledge of their past could assure. Thus, in 1921, after receiving his B.A. degree, Hansberry issued the following printed statement: "Announcing an Effort to Promote the Study and Facilitate the Teaching of the Fundamentals of NEGRO LIFE AND HISTORY."* This announcement explained that Hansberry would visit several schools and colleges that summer (1921) "in an attempt to bring to the attention of teachers and students the signifi-

---

* A pamphlet in Hansberry's private papers (HPP).

cance of ancient African civilization." His immediate objectives were to stimulate formal studies of Africa, to secure funds to publish source books for school use, and to establish a bureau to promote popular interest in black studies through magazines, lectures, visual aids, and other sources. His longer-range objective was twofold: to prepare black leaders to become knowledgeable about their past and world affairs; and to build black pride and confidence.

This interest led Hansberry to develop a "plan for expanding a pioneer project in collegiate education." In 1922, Howard University, in response to correspondence from Hansberry, authorized the establishment of a series of courses on "Negro Civilizations of Ancient Africa"; and Hansberry, after having taught a year at Straight College in New Orleans, joined Howard University to inaugurate these courses as part of an African Civilization Section of the History Department. Within two years he had established the following three courses in which more than eight hundred students had enrolled:*

1) NEGRO PEOPLES IN THE CULTURES AND CIVILIZATIONS OF PREHISTORIC AND PROTO-HISTORIC TIMES. This was a survey course based on the latest archaeological and anthropological findings concerning the Paleolithic and Neolithic cultures of Africa, the pre-dynastic civilization of Ancient Egypt, and relations to the protohistoric and early historic civilizations of the eastern Mediterranean, and western and southern Asia.

2) THE ANCIENT CIVILIZATIONS OF ETHIOPIA. This course was a survey from about 4000 B.C., covering the general areas encompassed by the present-day countries of Sudan and Ethiopia. Hansberry relied on Egyptian, Hebrew, and Greek sources as well as archaeological and anthropological

*Hansberry's scrapbook, referred to hereafter as HS.

data from several expeditions, including the Harvard-Boston Expedition at Kerma, Napata, and Meroë.

3) THE CIVILIZATION OF WEST AFRICA IN MEDIEVAL AND EARLY MODERN TIMES. This course surveyed the political and cultural developments of Ghana, Mali, Songhai, and Yorubaland as portrayed in Arab chronicles, and the archaeological and anthropological evidence of English, French, and German investigations.

To teach these courses today would require tremendous preparation, source materials, and energy; in the 1920s the task was even more monumental. But Hansberry had begun to identify and acquire the necessary materials while at Harvard, and was able to launch his program with source materials that several universities lack even today. His bibliography included the principal Arabic works, in English or French translation, as well as those originally written in Western languages. In addition, Professor Hansberry, with the cooperation of the Geology Department, produced hundreds of slides (over 200 by 1925) to illustrate various aspects of his courses. Extensive use was made of maps and charts. Within two years, Hansberry had equipped an office and workshop sufficient for his classes. But to do so had required the generous cooperation also of the Library of Congress, the Anthropological and Archaeological sections of the Smithsonian Institution, and the libraries at Harvard. In all of these efforts, including the use of various translators, he was forced to rely heavily on his personal funds.

In June, 1925, Hansberry's African Civilization Section of the History Department sponsored a symposium on "The Cultures and Civilizations of Negro Peoples in Africa."* This pioneer effort presented twenty-eight scholarly papers by his students, including some from Panama, British Guiana (now

* Program in HPP.

Guyana), and Colombia. On view at the symposium were fossil finds and various archaeological objects. Indeed, Howard University and Professor Hansberry would seem to have been well on the way to carving out a very special niche in African studies.

But the 1920s also witnessed some deep disappointments. Shortly after he inaugurated the program, Professor Hansberry had to withstand attempts by some of his colleagues to discredit him personally and professionally. Two of Howard's most distinguished professors reported to J. Stanley Durkee, Howard University's last white president (1918–26), that Hansberry "was endangering the standards and reputation of the university by teaching matters for which there is no foundation in fact."* They also questioned Hansberry's ability to coordinate the African studies program. Based on this report, President Durkee and the board of trustees voted to discontinue Hansberry's program; but subsequent appeals, from where it is still not clear, persuaded the president and board to rescind their earlier decision. However, during the remainder of Durkee's administration financial and moral support were no longer given. In spite of this, Hansberry expressed no antagonism against his adversaries; instead, he simply explained that it was their ignorance of the African heritage that caused them to make their baseless charges.†

Neither the doubts of some colleagues nor the lack of strong support by the university deterred Hansberry. He continued to develop a program which required financial support greater than the administration at Howard provided. In June, 1927, for example, Professor Hansberry in a report to the administration expressed the belief "that no other department has achieved so much in proportion to University funds expended for the past five years—$50."‡ He

---

* From a report also in HPP.
† HPP
‡ HS

appealed to the administration to support his efforts so that Howard could achieve a "unique and superior distinction in the academic world in the immediate future." But as late as 1935, Hansberry wrote the dean that "I no longer can personally finance the cost for materials." He then requested funds to purchase a book on "the remarkable 'finds' by [L. S. B.] Leakey."° In September, 1935, Hansberry told the Howard President, Mordecai Johnson, that "I feel very strongly that my efforts and the cause of Negro History as I have tried to promote it at Howard University deserve better from the University."†

Those early years were indeed difficult financially and psychologically; but they were also the gestation period of African studies at Howard University; and Professor Hansberry was young, ambitious, and determined. He was particularly encouraged in his endeavors by the response of his students, not only because of their enthusiastic enrollment in his elective courses, but also because of the expense many of them undertook to purchase various kinds of illustrative materials. The public response was also gratifying. Hansberry received letters of commendation from persons across the country: from Canada, Portugal, the Harvard Anthropology Department, and the editor of the *Scientific American*. In addition, favorable comments were reported in *The Nation* of New York, *The Southwestern Christian Advocate* of New Orleans, and *The Tribune* of Georgetown, British Guiana.

Encouragement such as this buttressed Professor Hansberry's high aspirations for his program and the university. Indeed, he began to formulate "a plan for expanding a pioneer project in collegiate education." He called it, "Varia Africana Plan for Howard University."‡ This was a proposal in which, Hansberry explained, "there is no dearth of pub-

° Letter to Dean E. P. Davis, May 7, 1935
† Letter to Mordecai Johnson, September 17, 1935
‡ HPP

lished information about Africa; the published literature is most abundant. But the general public knows very little of those publications and their content. This is also true of many specialists who are required to formulate and express opinions about the achievements of Negro people."

Hansberry cited four key reasons for this state of affairs: 1) The information "has never been made accessible to the public." 2) It was technical in character and was written for specialists. 3) Most of the historical data were collected and described incidentally, or were indirectly concerned with African history, and to extract from these required a working knowledge of the basic principles and techniques of the specialists and their nomenclature. 4) The many national origins of the authors meant that much of the data appeared in a variety of languages, including Amharic, Arabic, Ethiopic, Coptic and Syriac.

However, Hansberry did not regard the problems as being insurmountable. He stressed the need to assemble, correlate, simplify, and make the material readable and accessible to the public. He listed some of the great repositories which would have to be visited: Widener Library, Harvard; Bodleian and Ashmolean at Oxford; British Museum; F. L. Griffith Library at Boars' Hill (England); Bibliothèque nationale, Paris; Königlische Bibliothek, Berlin; the Oriental Institute, University of Chicago; and the Library of Congress. During his lifetime he visited all but one of these libraries.

Hansberry believed that his "Varia Africana" would make Howard University capable of revolutionizing the old and deeply ingrained misconceptions about Africa, Africans, and black people generally. He noted: "No institution is more obligated and no Negro school is in a better position to develop such a program as Howard. No institution has access to specialized libraries—the Moorland Collection [at Howard], and city repositories; no where else are the thought and planning put forth; no better courses exist anywhere else; there are no better trained students anywhere, by virtue of racial background. This is the area in which Howard has the most promising and immediate opportunity to distinguish itself as a leader in the general cause of public enlightenment."*

Thus, long before the era of black studies and academic black power demands for community control of education and the development of curricula to meet the needs of Afro-Americans, Professor Hansberry perceived of Howard University as the vanguard of black education. To help realize that goal, he submitted several proposals to foundations to finance his projects. His first major proposal was submitted to The Spelman Fund, July 11, 1929. Extracts from that proposal not only reveal Hansberry's keen perspectives and goals in the area of African studies, but also reveal the revolutionary character of his plan for education at Howard University. He proposed to show that:

1) "Africa rather than Asia was in all probability the birthplace of the human race," and that "it was they [Africans], it appears, who first learned and then taught the rest of mankind how to make and use tools, to develop a religion, to practice art, to domesticate animals, to smelt metals— particularly iron, and to create and maintain a deliberately constructed and tradition-bound . . . state;"†

2) that dessication of the Sahara and Libyan deserts caused "the autochtonous Negroids and Negroes . . . to emigrate to Europe and Asia;"‡

3) that "many of the peoples and cultures of Ancient Egypt originated in equatorial Africa;"

4) that "the peoples of Ethiopia . . . vied with the mighty Assyrian Empire for the position of first place among the great organized world powers of that age;"

5) that "Ghana, Melle, Songhay, Nupe, were larger in

---

* HPP.

† This is now a generally accepted point of view.

‡ See also Chester Chand, "Implications of Early Human Migrations from Africa to Europe," *Man*, August, 1963, vol. 63, No. 152, p. 124.

size, more effectively organized, and higher in culture than most of the contemporary states of the Anglo-Saxon, the Germanic, and the Slavic regions of Europe," and that "increased dessication of the Sahara, the introduction of the Mohammedan religion and the Islamic systems of polity, and the establishment of the Arab, Berber, and European systems of slave trading brought on the disintegration of these Negro states and their civilizations."

Hansberry concluded his proposal by expressing the hope that his efforts at Howard would arouse "Negro peoples in particular to make a specific effort to revive and develop to the full those creative and spiritual powers which . . . are Nature's pre-eminent gifts to the African."*

Professor Hansberry's stated objectives were clearly "at odds with prevailing notions about Africa's past," to use his own assessment; not all of these are universally accepted even today. In any case, he eventually received a modest fellowship from the General Education Board, which enabled him to continue limited research at Harvard University (1929–30) while on sabbatical leave from Howard.

Although he failed to secure additional funds from Howard or elsewhere to supplement the small fellowship, Hansberry was reassured in his work by the sources he examined at Harvard and the patient support of his adviser, Professor Earnest A. Hooton, chairman of Harvard's Anthropology Department. After completing his sabbatical at Harvard, Hansberry returned to Howard where he strengthened his courses on Africa, enlarged the library holdings, and rededicated himself in efforts to secure sufficient funds for developing his program and publishing the much needed source books.

Although in 1923 he had corresponded with Professor F. L. Griffith, a distinguished Egyptologist, who complimented his work and expressed the hope of seeing him if he

---

* *A Proposal for Funds,* July 11, 1929, p. 11.

visited England, it was during the early 1930s that Hansberry entered into extensive correspondence with several well-known European scholars about his courses at Howard and the research he wanted to continue in preparation for source books. E. A. Wallis Budge, of the British Museum and an early authority on Egypt, Ethiopia, and the eastern Sudan, encouraged Hansberry to pursue his work in England and offered his assistance; A. H. Sayce, a philologist at Oxford, offered his counsel and recommended others Hansberry could contact; E. L. Collie, curator at the Logan Museum, encouraged Hansberry to pursue his stated aims; Sir W. M. Flinders Petrie, another renowned Egyptologist, offered his help; C. G. Seligmann, the Oxford anthropologist, offered his counsel; and L. P. Kirwan, an archaeologist at Oxford, agreed to serve as his adviser if he went to Oxford.*

Hansberry began seeking opportunities for field work in Africa. In 1932 he learned that Professor Griffith was planning to lead an expedition to the Sudan. The young Hansberry, therefore, diplomatically sought the counsel of two trusted advisers, Dows Dunham at the Museum of Fine Arts (Boston), and Professor Hooton, on whether or not his being black might disqualify his joining the expedition. I have been unable to find a response from Hooton on this subject, but Dunham said in part:

> To be perfectly frank with you, if I were in charge of such an expedition, I should hesitate long before taking an American Negro on my staff. . . . I should fear that the mere fact of your being a member of the staff would seriously affect the prestige of the other members and the respect which the native employees would have for them. . . . I feel sure

* Letter file, HPP: Budge to Hansberry, January 29, 1932; Griffith to Hansberry, February 6, 1923; Sayce to Hansberry, February 11, 1932; Collie to Hansberry, November 8, 1928; Petrie to Hansberry, February 10, 1932; Seligmann to Hansberry, September 30, 1936; and Kirwan to Hansberry, September 29, 1936; and notes in the scrapbook, p. 12.

that you know me well enough to realize that I do not say this out of any feeling of race prejudice.*

Hansberry did not accompany the expedition; and I have nothing to suggest that he was discouraged by Dunham's reply (which he probably anticipated), or that he ever used the incident to rationalize his limited success during those early years. He continued to seek funds for his program at Howard and for his own research. Finally, the General Education Board awarded him a fellowship to study at Oxford. Hansberry prepared for that opportunity by pursuing independent research in African history and archaeology at the University of Chicago in 1936.

At Oxford (1937–38) Hansberry worked with L. P. Kirwan, who was director of the Oxford Expedition to Nubia. It appeared that at last Professor Hansberry had received his golden opportunity of working under an expert archaeologist, and in Sudan! For in their previous exchange of letters, Kirwan was impressed by Hansberry's proposal for study in England, Egypt, and Sudan, though he did express some concern about the petitioner's "limited training" in archaeology. As it turned out, however, Kirwan attempted to steer Hansberry away from his initial proposal. In fact, he later suggested a project which Hansberry might conduct out of Boston! But Hansberry was determined. With no prospect of joining Kirwan's expedition to Sudan, Hansberry pursued what research he could at Oxford, and consulted with several other authorities, including long discussions with A. J. Arkell, who was on leave at Oxford from his post as Director of Antiquities for the Sudan.†

Hansberry's project proposed a historical reinterpretation of archaeological work in Ethiopia and Nubia between the eighth century B.C. and the sixth century A.D. He especially wanted to study more recent evidence and apply modern techniques in the re-examination of the conclusions

* Letter file HPP, Dunham to Hansberry, February 2, 1932.
† HS.

reached by Herman Junker, whose article, "The First Appearance of the Negroes in History" (*Journal of Egyptian Archaeology*, 1921, VII) maintains that Egyptians and neighboring people of the Sudan are not Negroid but Hamites (Caucasians). The answer as to whether or not Kirwan's attempts to dissuade Hansberry from pursuing the project were personal or professional must await additional research. Hansberry's report to the General Education Board was that his project closely paralleled one under consideration by Kirwan himself. In any case, the Howard professor remained steadfast, and completed his year's study at Oxford.

In 1938 he returned from his Oxford studies and continued to expand his program at Howard. At this time he was promoted to assistant professor (sixteen years after his initial appointment). Although his Oxford experience had not been as rewarding as he had hoped, he was more convinced than ever that his research efforts had to be continued. Consequently, he revised and expanded his research proposal, received the counsel of Hooton at Harvard and W. F. Albright, an anthropologist at the Johns Hopkins University, and in 1947 submitted his project to the Rosenwald and Carnegie Foundations. It was in this connection that Hooton wrote his much quoted letter in Hansberry's behalf:

> I am quite confident that no present-day scholar has anything like the knowledge of this field (prehistory of Africa) that Hansberry has developed. He has been unable to take the Ph.D. degree . . . because there is no university or institution . . . that has manifested a really profound interest in this subject.*

Albright had written President Mordecai Johnson earlier: "What was my pleasure . . . to find that Mr. Hansberry had covered the ground with extraordinary thoroughness and competence."†

---

* Hooton to W. W. Alexander (Rosenwald Fund), September 17, 1948, found in HPP.
† Albright to Mordecai Johnson, January 6, 1947, found in HPP.

In spite of this support, the intercession of some Howard University officials, and an extensively detailed project with evidence that several stages of the study were nearing completion, Hansberry was denied financial support by both foundations. This latest setback, coming twenty-five years after he had inaugurated the African studies program at Howard with great personal and financial sacrifices, was no doubt one of Hansberry's greatest disappointments.

But this pioneering Africanist was relentless. As African studies became more popular during the post World War II era, Hansberry began to receive some of the recognition due him. In 1953 he became a Fulbright Research Scholar in Egypt and for the next year he engaged in field work there, in the Republic of Sudan, and in Ethiopia. He also gave lectures to academic and general audiences in several African countries during that year.

Ironically, it was during Hansberry's leave as Fulbright Scholar that Howard University received a Ford Foundation grant to develop a program of African studies. Hansberry was neither included in any of the decisions relating to those developments nor was he even informed that such discussions were underway. His feelings about this are best described by him:

> While in Liberia, the last country visited during my extensive African travels in 1954, I learned from one of my former students—for the first time and to my great surprise— that the University was establishing a program of African Studies under the direction of the Head of the Department of Sociology. Since I had been engaged in a program of African Studies at the University for more than thirty years, it was difficult for me to understand why I had received— during my year abroad—no official word concerning this unusual development. On my return to the University I learned that the program had been made possible by a substantial grant in funds by the Ford Foundation under arrangements which excluded my courses in African Studies from the program and therefore from any of the benefits

accruing from the grant. In view of my years of service which I had given—at much personal sacrifice—to the effort to establish a broadly based program of African Studies at Howard and taking into account the wide recognition which I had received for these endeavors from agencies outside the University, it is needless to say that the University's attitude in this matter was not a particularly enheartening experience.*

To attempt an unraveling of the complex developments that led to the situation described above is a precarious endeavor. It is clear that Professor Hansberry was excluded from the initial consultations and planning for the new African Studies Program although his ideas served as a guide for it; it is less clear, however, what his role was in the program during subsequent years. Rayford W. Logan, former chairman of the Department of History at Howard University, has written that the program was administered by an Interdepartmental Committee including, among others, himself, Hansberry, and E. Franklin Frazier, who served for several years as chairman.† One would assume that this meant the endorsement of Hansberry's courses by the committee at some point, if not at the outset. But whatever the case, Hansberry did not play a major role in the program although he had already devoted over thirty years to academic and experiential preparation in the field, a credential few American scholars could claim. One should also note that while Howard was withholding this recognition from Hansberry, several persons and organizations outside the university not only recognized his achievements but sought his counsel on Africa; his distinctions were crowned by the African Research Award from the Haile Selassie I Prize

---

* This appears on a page in Hansberry's scrapbook. There is no evidence that it was sent to anyone and is undated.
† Rayford W. Logan, *Howard University: The First Hundred Years* (New York: New York University Press, 1969), pp. 436, 540.

Trust in 1964. Very likely, then, Hansberry's peripheral role in the new program resulted from politics within the university, which have not yet been evaluated.

By the 1950s Hansberry's contribution to the study of Africa at Howard included five courses: "Peoples and Cultures of Africa in Stone Age Times"; "Culture and Political History of Nilotic Lands in Historical Antiquity"; "Cultural and Political History of Kushite or Ethiopian Lands in the Middle Ages"; "Cultural and Political History of the Kingdoms and Empires of the Western Sahara and the Western Sudan"; and "Archaeological Methods and Materials." Not only does an examination of the available syllabi, notes, and lectures convince one of the incredible number of diverse sources Professor Hansberry used, or the tremendous scope of his courses; but one is equally impressed by the fact that he concentrated his efforts in ancient and medieval times. In 1957, in addition to teaching at Howard, Professor Hansberry became a lecturer on early African civilizations at the New School for Social Research in New York.

Professor Hansberry retired from Howard in 1959. He ended his teaching career among the peoples and lands of Africa. The University of Nigeria, which awarded him the doctorate of letters in 1961, established in his name the Hansberry Institute of African Studies. In September, 1963, the former Howard professor became a Distinguished Visiting Professor at the University of Nigeria where he gave the inaugural address for the Hansberry Institute. Symbolically, only a few hundred miles away in Africa (Ghana) and just a few weeks previously, Hansberry's great mentor, W. E. B. Du Bois, had died (in August, 1963) while still actively engaged in African studies.

One of the most important aspects of Professor Hansberry's academic career was the enthusiastic response and support of his students. Perhaps his first great joy in this regard came when he entered his class to the cheers of his students, after the Howard University president and board of trustees reversed their decision to discontinue his courses in the 1920s. He gave untiringly of his time to all of his students; but he assumed a particular interest in the African students. Hansberry realized that the African students not only had to contend with life in this racist country, but that they also had the obligation to return to their countries with both the skills acquired at Howard, and an Afro-centric perspective of their heritage. It was in this latter connection, through his courses and personal contacts, that Hansberry made his great contribution to African students, dispelling the derogatory myths and stereotypes about their culture and affirming their dignity, pride, and sense of achievement among the peoples of the world.

In 1946 Professor Hansberry was appointed Faculty Adviser to African students, and in 1950 he was appointed to Howard's Emergency Aid to the African Students Committee. The latter assignment concerned African scholarships and related financial matters. Both positions seemed to merge with Hansberry's personal concern for the general welfare of African students, who continually brought a multitude of private and university matters for him to resolve. Hansberry accepted those responsibilities without extra compensation or additional clerical assistance. But his correspondence increased two- or threefold. Letters were written in response to queries from Africa about admissions and financial aid for students; replies were sent to African parents inquiring about a student's academic and social problems; petitions were submitted to foundations for student aid; recommendations were written for students to enter graduate or professional school; and in at least one case, extensive and detailed correspondence was undertaken in connection with an African student's death. Much of the cost of all this was paid for by Professor Hansberry.

In another instance, Hansberry wrote President W. V. S. Tubman of Liberia to reinstate a student's scholarship (a student who later became a highly placed public official in Liberia). There is correspondence relating to several thousand dollars which Emperor Haile Selassie of Ethiopia contributed to the Committee on Aid to African Students.* In 1958 Professor Hansberry recorded that over $24,000 had been made available to African students from sources outside Howard University.

Up to the 1960s Howard University still had the largest African student enrollment in the country, and most of those students received scholarship assistance. While some countries made contributions, Ethiopia and Liberia, for example, most of the aid during the 1950s came from the Scholarship Committee of the African-American Institute (A.A.I.). In 1951, for instance, African students received A.A.I. grants at thirty-seven American institutions: fourteen were at Howard University; five were at Harvard; and three each at Cornell and Ohio Wesleyan. Between October, 1957, and January, 1959, Hansberry's records show that $8,099.00 were contributed as grants to African students at Howard. Most of this resulted from the initiative and efforts of Professor Hansberry, who was appointed to the A.A.I. Scholarship Committee in 1959.

With the increased interest of the United States government in Africa and Africans during the 1950s, Hansberry's role with students became even more important as a fund raiser, counselor (many referred to him as father), and teacher. He was instrumental in the organization of the African Students Association of the United States and Canada, and in 1951, 1959, and 1963 he received that organization's Award of Honor. Recognition and thanks also came over the years in many letters from former students and their parents. One former student wrote in 1958 that he had started a "Hansberry Club" at the Queen's Royal College in

---

* Letters on these and many other matters abound in the Hansberry private papers.

the West Indies.* A study of the high esteem Hansberry's students had for him would indeed constitute an important and moving chapter of one of America's most dedicated Africanists.

Although the number and identity of everyone who benefited from Professor Hansberry's counsel and assistance will never be known, it is certain, however, that such beneficiaries were not limited to former students. His papers are full of references to materials sent or lent to colleagues, friends, and others who requested them. In addition, friends and relatives recall how Hansberry spent hours discussing various aspects of African history with persons who subsequently established themselves in print in fields relating to Africa. Hansberry sent references to W. E. B. Du Bois in 1933 and also provided materials to help Du Bois prepare a course on ancient Africa at Atlanta University in 1936. This Du Bois greatly appreciated, and he, unlike many lesser scholars, readily acknowledged the value of Hansberry's work and encouraged him to continue it. In the Foreword of his book, *The World and Africa*, Du Bois noted that: ". . . of greatest help to me has been Leo Hansberry." Professor Hansberry also counseled and sent syllabi, bibliographies, visual aids, and other materials to Edwin Smith, who, in 1943, was organizing African studies at Fisk University.†

Hansberry also corresponded and had personal contacts with many African political leaders, including A. J. Luthuli, the black South African who won the Nobel Peace Award for 1960, and J. Boakye Danquah, the Ghanaian lawyer who headed the United Gold Coast Convention party. In 1955 Danquah wrote to Hansberry requesting information on ancient Ghana.‡ He had read Du Bois's *The World and*

---

* Letter file, HPP, Neville Clarke to Hansberry, March 15, 1958.
† Letter file, HPP, Smith to Hansberry, September 22, 1943.
‡ Letter file, HPP, Lituli [sic] to Hansberry, 1961; Danquah to Hansberry, May 28, 1956.

Africa and had seen where the latter had relied on Hansberry for data regarding Ethiopia and Egypt. He also requested a copy of Delafosse's *The Negroes of Africa* and any publication by Hansberry himself, which he evidently received, since in a letter dated May 28, 1956, Danquah expressed thanks for Hansberry's "Africa and the Western World," *The Midwest Journal*, 1955, Vol. VII.

Despite his difficulties and his tremendous teaching and counseling duties, Professor Hansberry found the time and energy to publish. In addition to book reviews and review articles which appeared in the *Journal of Negro Education*, *Africa Special Report, Panorama,* and the *Washington Post* newspaper, Professor Hansberry wrote many articles that were unusual for their time because few people were writing seriously in this field. Most of those who wrote focused on a more recent period. They were also unusual because they revealed Hansberry's wide familiarity with diverse sources in various languages. Some of these were as follows:

"Sources for the Study of Ethiopian History," *Howard University Studies in History*, 1930, vol. II;

"A Negro in Anthropology," *Opportunity*, 1933, vol. XI;

"African Studies," *Phylon*, 1944, vol. V;

"Imperial Ethiopia in Ancient Times," *The Ethiopian Review* (Addis Ababa, Ethiopia: August, 1944), vol. I;

"Ethiopia in the Middle Ages," *The Ethiopian Review* (September and November, 1944), vol. 1;

"The Historical Background of African Art," *Howard University Gallery of Art*, 1953;

"Africa and the Western World," *The Midwest Journal*, 1955, vol. VII;

"Indigenous African Religions," *Africa Seen by American Negro Scholars* (Présence Africaine, 1958);

"Ancient Kush, Old Ethiopia and the Balad es Sudan," *Journal of Human Relations*, 1960, vol. VIII;

"Africa: The World's Richest Continent," *Freedomways,*
1963, vol. III;

Africana at Nsukka (Viking Press, 1964);

"Ethiopian Ambassadors to Latin Courts and Latin Emissaries to Prester John," *Ethiopia Observer* (Ethiopia and
Britain, 1965), vol. IX, no. 2;

"W. E. B. Du Bois's Influence on African History," *Freedomways,* 1965, vol. V, no. 1.

Although seldom mentioned in connection with political
activities, Hansberry's involvement in African issues did indeed extend into various political arenas. In fact, one may
argue that the fulfillment of his commitment to the unpopular effort "to bring to the attention of teachers and students the significance of ancient African civilization" required political activities. Professor Hansberry believed that
all persons of African descent needed to know the richness
of their past and appreciate the great potential for the present and future. He regarded African studies as a necessary
means to develop or maintain black pride and confidence in
a world dominated politically, economically, and culturally
by whites. However, he was by no stretch of the imagination
a racist; he believed in racial harmony; but he also believed
that a prerequisite for that harmony was a fuller apprecia-
tion of the black heritage. This resulted in his plans for a
"pioneer project in collegiate education," and his efforts to
educate the public in general. His attempts to reorient America's racial perspectives by destroying the old myths and
stereotypes had to assume political implications; his difficulties at Howard confirm this at the university level.

But Hansberry also took very deliberate political courses
of action at the national and international levels. As early
as the Fourth Pan-African Conference (New York, 1927) the
young Hansberry began to make his knowledge available for
the mobilization of African peoples. At that conference he

discussed the archaeological history of Africa and its significance for blacks. In 1934, Hansberry and others organized the Ethiopian Research Council, of which he became director, and William M. Steen, secretary. The objectives of the council were to stimulate American interest in Ethiopia's efforts to resist the Italian invasion, and to disseminate information on Ethiopian history, ancient and modern. Correspondents were located in London, Paris, Rome, and Addis Ababa; affiliates were listed in Ethiopia, France, and Panama, in addition to Chicago, New York, and Philadelphia. Associates included Afro-Americans, a Ugandan, a Nigerian, and some Ethiopians. Ralph Bunche served as Advisor on International Law.*

Although it is difficult at this stage of research to determine the extent of the council's success, it is noteworthy that in 1936, Count Ciano, the Italian Minister of Foreign Affairs, informed the U.S. State Department of Italy's displeasure and concern over a plan for Emperor Haile Selassie to visit the United States. The count's communication identified Hansberry as director of the group sponsoring the visit "for propaganda purposes."† It is also worthy of note that during the 1940s, after the emperor regained his throne, Hansberry assisted the Ethiopian ambassador in recruiting teachers and technicians.‡ These activities merit additional research.

In the 1950s the United States took an increasingly serious interest in Africa, and among persons invited to testify before the Senate Foreign Relations Committee to discuss the Point Four program (foreign aid) was Professor Hansberry. He stressed the need for the following: provisions to help African organizations, corporations, and businessmen

---

* HS; also a letter written on Ethiopian Research Council stationery dated June, 1936, listing officers, advisers and affiliates, found in HPP.
† *Foreign Relations of the United States, The Near East and Africa*, 1936, vol. 3, p. 218.
‡ HS.

make direct application for financial and technical aid; educational provisions to train Africans; and provisions for funds to non-self-governing African territories. He also referred to Howard University's success in training Africans. While there is no way to assess the impact of his testimony, it is important that his expertise was sought by the government and that his suggestions showed that he perceived Africa's pressing needs.

In 1952 a group that included William Steen, James Grant, Robert W. Williams, Jr., Henrietta Van Noy, and Hansberry organized the Institute of African-American Relations to further understanding of Africa and to improve relations with Africans. The institute published *The African-American Bulletin*. Shortly after founding the institute, Hansberry and other members entered into discussions with several groups interested in Africa. The result was the organization of the African-American Institute (A.A.I.), where Hansberry served as a trustee. As one of its activities the A.A.I. sponsored Africa House (Washington, D.C.) as a home base for African students in the United States. Given that concern, there was hardly any person better suited to administer Africa House than Professor Hansberry, who became chairman of its governing council. The All-African Student Union of the Americas had its offices there, and this contributed to the lively concerns and diverse programs of Africa House.

Professor Hansberry's long and dedicated experience with African studies and students won him tremendous respect, among Africans in particular. His many contacts helped him to maintain at Africa House a program which was both substantive and timely. There were lectures, seminars, movies, slides, exhibits, field trips, dances, and receptions. Among the guests who were honored at Africa House were Prime Minister Sylvanus Olympio of Togo; Chief Justice Kobina Arku-Korsah of Ghana; President Sekou Touré of Guinea; and Alioune Diop, Director of the

Society of African Culture (Paris). Indeed, for the 1950s and early 1960s, Hansberry developed an impressive program for Africa House.* As noted earlier, Hansberry also served on A.A.I.'s Scholarship Committee. Future research on Hansberry's influence in A.A.I. would no doubt prove very revealing.

This profile of Professor Hansberry would be remiss without some mention of his readiness to speak for social groups and counsel the layman about Africa. His private correspondence is replete with references to these kinds of activities. He was often an underpaid (or unpaid) but welcome speaker for church groups, school organizations, community clubs, lodges, and student groups. Many times after giving a talk, Hansberry would be asked for a copy of his speech, a list of books, or a copy of a syllabus; and he usually complied with such requests. Although justice can not be done in evaluating this aspect of Hansberry's activities until further research is undertaken, it is already clear that he was, in a very real sense, a peoples' professor. Indeed, the fact that Hansberry often delayed his research and writing to make himself available for a discussion of Africa with anyone so interested, is a basic justification for publishing his *Notebook* for the general reader. Such a publication of his works for this audience probably honors him at least as much as any of the several awards he received in life.

Professor Hansberry's honors include three Awards of Honor from the African Student Association of the United States and Canada (1951, 1959, 1963); a bronze citation for "Forty Years of Service in the Cause of African Freedom," from the United Friends of Africa (1961); an Achievement Award from The Omega Psi Phi Fraternity (1961); the first African Research Award from the Haile Selassie I Prize

* HS.

Trust (1964); the LL.D. degree by Virginia State College and the Litt.D. degree by the University of Nigeria (both in 1961); and the LL.D. by Morgan State College (1965).

A few comments should be made about Professor Hansberry's views on African historiography. He spent most of his professional career attempting to rescue African history from the denigrated status Europeans had established for it. He observed that the custom had developed to associate Ethiopia and Europe in much the same way as the expressions "Negro" and "Nordic," the former being considered inferior to the latter. Hansberry thus dedicated himself to the task of showing that this popular conception was historically ill-founded, a central theme of much of his writings.

Professor Hansberry was fascinated by the obsession of early European writers with Ethiopia. The designation itself was "distinctly a European product, for no Africans referred to themselves as Ethiopians or their country as Ethiopia until after Europeans coined the label;"* and neither ancient Egyptians nor Hebrews referred to Africans by those terms. Hansberry noted that the first writer to employ the terms seems to have been Homer, in his ninth-century B.C. work, the *Iliad*. In time, the designations Ethiopia and Ethiopians became perhaps more widespread and commonly known than those of any other land and people of ancient times. Hansberry wrote:

> It is a curious fact that centuries before the geographical and historical terms Babylon, Assyria, Persia, Carthage, and Etruria, or for that matter Greece and Rome themselves, had made their first appearance in the writings of classical authors, Ethiopia was already an old and familiar expression; and long after the names Babylon, Assyria, Carthage, and Etruria had become scarcely more than

---

* The Greeks and Romans applied the term Ethiopian to the several dark or black ethnic groups in Africa; the description, therefore, bore no necessary relationship to the present country of that name.

vague memories, preserved only in the morgue of history, the hoary designation "Ethiopia" continued in use.*

As a student and teacher of Greek history also, he observed that Europe's earliest poetry, geography, and history memorialized Ethiopia and Ethiopians; the great classical writers—Homer, Hesiod, Herodotus, Aeschylus, Sophocles, Euripides, Diodorus, Pliny the Elder, and others—contributed greatly to the internationalization of those designations and helped to establish them as among the "oldest living terms" in European literature.

The reasons for this long, continuous European preoccupation with Ethiopia have puzzled many historians for centuries. Undoubtedly, however, the meaning of the term itself—land of the sun-burned or black-faced men—is an important key. It referred to and indeed reflected a sensitivity to people of black complexion. Professor Snowden has emphasized this point:

> Color was obviously uppermost in the minds of the Greeks and Romans, whether they were describing Ethiopians in the land of their origin or their expatriated congeners in Egypt, Greece, or Italy. The distinguishing mark of an Ethiopian was the color of his skin.†

However, the more crucial questions are what that sensitivity meant in ancient times, and to what extent it influenced the personal attitudes of subsequent eras.

Some historians see in much of the classical literature the genesis of denigratory racial and color attitudes and concepts. In defense of that conclusion, they cite such classical

---

* Undated manuscript in HPP.

† The most recent and thorough evaluative synthesis in this area is Frank Snowden, *Blacks in Antiquity: Ethiopians in the Greco-Roman Experience* (Cambridge, Massachusetts; Harvard University Press, 1970). Snowden and Hansberry were colleagues and friends at Howard University for many years. Another valuable book is Grace H. Beardsley, *The Negro in Greek and Roman Civilization: A Study of the Ethiopian Type* (Baltimore and London, 1929).

descriptions of Ethiopians as "mysterious, with tightly curled or woolly hair, broad and flattened noses, thick and puffy lips." Herodotus characterized their speech as resembling "the shrieking of a bat rather than the language of men." Pliny the Elder described them as having "by report . . . no heads but mouth and eyes in their breast." The proverbial expression, "to wash an Ethiopian white," falls into the same stereotypic pattern. Black is associated with dirt that cannot be washed white (clean). The label, "man-eating Aeothiopians," further stereotyped black people. Whatever the intent and whether conscious or not, these critics point to the classical writers as purveyors of racist germs.

On the other hand, there are critics, including Professor Hansberry, who have emphasized that stream of ancient description which characterized the Ethiopians as "pious and just." While Snowden's book cites much of the information included in the above paragraph, he concludes: "Classical texts have often been misinterpreted because scholars have mistakenly attributed to antiquity racial attitudes and concepts which derive from certain modern views regarding the Negro." Hansberry shared that point of view (and may have discussed it with his long-time friend and colleague) and believed that an acquaintance with the "real position of ancient Ethiopians in early European tradition would provide correctives to the opprobious and mistaken connotations" related to Africans, "connotations which certain historical and social developments have caused to become almost universally accepted as the genuine and original characterizations." In short, Professor Hansberry sought to rehabilitate "that attitude of mind which prevailed in the lands and among the peoples who originated the terms Ethiopia and Ethiopians as designations of a culture and people which they knew at first hand."*

It should be emphasized that Professor Hansberry wrote

* Hansberry lecture notes, undated, HPP.

at a time when the academic and political vogue was "to prove" the black man's equality by presenting evidence of his culture and noting his contributions to world civilization. Hansberry not only has demonstrated such a contribution, he has revealed the very close contact and interrelationships that existed between ancient and medieval Africans, in this case, Ethiopians and Europeans. Based on his evaluation of those interactions, Hansberry concluded that the early Greeks and Romans regarded Ethiopians as full human beings. Such a conclusion meant that the explanation for the evolution of the concept of black inferiority had to be traced to some other source. And until recently the source was traced to the slave trade and slavery, a position Hansberry accepted. On the other hand, and somewhat ironically, Hansberry's research can also be used to suggest conscious or unconscious black derogation in ancient times. Indeed, changing times demand reinterpretation not only in terms of new data but also in terms of new perspectives, and no reputable historian would deny that; certainly Hansberry would not. In fact, for his generation Hansberry pioneered a reinterpretation of the African heritage.

The William Leo Hansberry
African History Notebook

I

The Queen of Sheba: A Source of National Identity in Ethiopia

The story of the Queen of Sheba is one of the most ubiquitous and compelling legends in history. It has been perpetuated in various parts of the world in literature, music, and paintings (Shakespeare's Henry VIII; *poems by Lascelles Abercrombie, Rudyard Kipling, and W. B. Yeats; musical pieces by Karl Goldmark, C. F. Gounod, and G. F. Handel; European and Persian paintings; and the Ethiopian tableau which portrays the story in forty-four vivid pictures). The essential components of the legend are derived from both Ethiopian and non-Ethiopian sources: the latter include the biblical accounts; the Koranic version, and supplements by Muslim commentators; and Jewish sources. The Ethiopian component of the legend is rooted in the* Kebra Nagast *and* Fatha Nagast *(royal Ethiopian chronicles), Axumite inscriptions, and oral traditions.*

The most important of the Ethiopian sources is the Kebra Nagast, *whose significance is minimized by some authorities because it appeared after the restoration in the fourteenth century of the Solomonic dynasty, which it justifies and identifies with the Queen of Sheba. Other authorities accept the explanation that the document is a translation of a source found early in the fourth century A.D. and is legitimate. Professor Hansberry accepted the latter position.*

The Queen of Sheba legend makes the Ethiopian monarchy both a physical and a religious descendant of the kingship of Israel; it also rooted the monarchy in the concept of divine kingship; and both of these ideas are embedded in the Ethiopian constitution of 1955. The strength of the legend is further revealed in the continuity of the Solomonic line, which is generally held to be the oldest surviving monarchy in the world, presently held since 1917 (as regent) and 1928 (as emperor) by Haile Selassie I, known also as the Conquering Lion of the Tribe of Judah and the Elect of God.

The veracity of the legend of Sheba is less important than the fact that it influenced the structure of Ethiopian society and helped to entrench in Ethiopian traditions a focus of national identity and unity by legitimizing the Solomonic dynasty. The extent to which these facts can be harmonized with contemporary times provides Ethiopia with a major challenge in the post World War II era.

While others have written on the subject—a recent and valuable book is Edward Ullendorff's, Ethiopia and the Bible *—the following Hansberry essay is valuable because of its point of view and the varied sources Hansberry presents.*

The Editor

No name or royal title relating to a woman of historical antiquity is more familiar to the learned and the laity of the Western world than is the Queen of Sheba. Traditions concerning her visit to King Solomon are infinitely better known than is the story of Jezebel's hapless adventure at Ahab's court and the stirring story of Queen Hatshepsut's famous expedition to Punt. Not even the thrilling romances woven around the love affairs of Aspasia and Pericles; Théodora and Justinian; or even Cleopatra and Marc Antony have attained wider popular fame.

But who was the Queen of Sheba and where was the kingdom over which she held royal sway? Ancient, medieval, and modern writers have never been able to arrive at a common answer to these questions. In Ethiopia it has long been all but universally believed that she was an Ethiopian queen named Makeda; and there have been a number of Western authors who have shared Ethiopian opinions in this respect. Among the ancients were Flavius Josephus, the famous Jewish historian, and such Fathers of the Church as Origen, Saint Anselm, and the great Saint Augustine. In the Middle Ages and early modern times those of similar opinions included the anonymous twelfth-century author of the *De Imagena Munda*, Abu Salih (the Armenian historian), and Fathers Francisco Alvarez, Alfonso Mendez, and Pedro Paez, as well as the noted seventeenth-century Portuguese historians, Father Toledo and Balthazar Telles. In more recent times the great explorer James Bruce, the noted missionary J. L. Krapf, the learned French historian Louis J. Morie, and —with reservations—Sir Wallis Budge, must be added to the list.

On the other hand, in ancient and medieval Palestine and medieval Arabia it was widely believed that the renowned Queen of Sheba was an ancient Arabian queen named Belkis and that the Yemenite Kingdom of Himyar was her ancestral domain. Ancient and medieval commentators who have concurred in this opinion include Saint Cyprian, Saint Justin the Martyr, Cyril of Alexandria, Epiphanius, and Cardinal Caesar Baronius.

How are these two conflicting points of view concerning the Queen of Sheba's identity and the whereabouts of her kingdom to be explained? The best way to answer this question is first to examine the great body of historical tradition out of which the divergent interpretations of the Sheba story have emerged. This vast mass of historical tradition falls naturally into three categories—first, traditions of Ethiopian origin; second, traditions recorded by rabbinical and Arabic authors in the Middle Ages; and third, the references to the Queen of Sheba in the Old and New Testaments. The traditions epitomized in the biblical references are much more widely known than are the others; but they are also the most enigmatic and the ones which have done most to evoke questions concerning the famous queen's identity and the geographical location of the kingdom over which she ruled. This is explained by the tantalizingly brief and inconclusive character of the references to not only the queen herself but to her domain as well. The longest and the least enigmatic of these references are the passages in Chapter Ten of the *First Book of Kings* in which the Queen of Sheba's visit to King Solomon is reported in some detail, but with fewer particulars than desired. From the relevant passage in that chapter we learn that:

> . . . when the Queen of Sheba heard of the fame of Solomon . . . she came to prove him with hard questions. And she came to Jerusalem with a very great train, with camels that bore spices, and very much gold and precious stones; and when she was come to Solomon she communed with him of all that was in her heart. . . . And she gave the king an hundred and twenty talents of gold, and of spices, very great store, and precious stones; there came no more such abundance of spices as those which the Queen of Sheba gave to King Solomon. . . . And King Solomon gave unto the Queen of Sheba all her desire, whatever she asked. . . . So she turned and went to her own country, she and her servants.

In Chapter Nine of the *Second Book of Chronicles*, a somewhat shorter but otherwise almost identical account of Sheba's visit to Solomon is recorded; but in neither of the accounts is there much on which to establish a definite identity, or the geographical region from which the Queen came and to which she returned. Nor in the other biblical references to a Queen who "came from the uttermost parts of the earth to hear the wisdom of Solomon"; it is generally agreed that these allusions are to the Queen of Sheba but in both references she is called simply the "Queen of the South."

In verse three, Chapter Forty-three of the *Book of Isaiah*, the land of Sheba is named, along with the lands of Kush and Egypt, in a context which implies that they were among the richest nations of the earth; and in verse six of Chapter Sixty of the same book there is another allusion to Sheba's great wealth. The *Book of Ezekiel* refers in Chapter Twenty-seven, verses twenty-two and twenty-three, to the "merchants of Sheba" who traded in the marts of Tyre in "all spices" and in "precious stones and gold"; and in verse Twenty, Chapter Six of *Jeremiah*, the land of Sheba is described as being "rich in incense." And, finally, in *The Book of Psalms*, Psalm Seventy-two, verse ten, in the famous allusion to a coming Messiah it is prophesied that on His arrival "the Kings of Tarshish and of the Isles" would bring Him presents and "the Kings of Sheba and Saba shall offer gifts." But as has already been implied, in none of these references nor in their context is there anything which makes it possible to point with absolute certainty to the geographical location of the land and Kingdom of Sheba.

Turning next to the Ethiopian traditions about King Solomon's queenly visitor, it may be said that they are far less marred by the tantalizing inconclusiveness which characterizes the biblical traditions. For Queen Mekeda, whom the Ethiopians identified as the biblical Queen of Sheba, is placed most emphatically within the boundaries of present-day Ethiopia; and so, of course, is the kingdom of which she was the sovereign ruler. In addition, this great body of tradition has preserved some very interesting particulars about the dynasty to which Queen Makeda belonged, about her parents, her personal history, and, above all, a remarkably detailed account of her visit to King Solomon and its immediate aftermath. Also, of considerable significance is the fact that these particulars and details are singularly free from obviously fictitious events and fabulous inventions of the sort which are altogether too frequent, as we shall presently see, in the traditions which rabbinical and medieval Arabic writers have endeavored to tie into the biblical account of King Solomon's famous visitor.

The biblical version of the Sheba story has been quite well known in the Western world ever since the Old and New Testaments were introduced with the establishment of the Christian church; but Christendom's acquaintance with the Makeda tradition of Ethiopia, even in an abridged form, dates back only a little over four hundred years. Perhaps the earliest significant digest of the story was that which appeared in Father Francisco Alvarez's famous history of the Portuguese embassy to Ethiopia between 1520 and 1526, and which was first published in Lisbon in 1540. During his sojourn in the country, Father Alvarez heard and recorded much about the ancient queen whom the Ethiopians equated with the biblical Queen of Sheba; and in accordance with prevailing tradition, Alvarez regarded the ruined town of Axum—where he spent eight months—as having been the site of Sheba's capital city.

Later Portuguese authors, such as Alfonso Mendez and Manuel d'Almeida, and others who visited the country between 1526 and 1630, acquired and published additional details which amplified and confirmed Father Alvarez's summary of the Ethiopian version of the Sheba story and her capital. Then came the new and particularly revealing version of the same story which was acquired in the main from the learned Ethiopian monk Abbé Gregoris by the great Job

Ludolphus, who included it in his famous *Historia Aethiopica*, which was first published in Frankfurt in 1681. Father Alvarez's digest had already become available to an ever-widening circle of readers through the translation and publication of his chronicle in Italian in 1550, French in 1556, Spanish in 1557, German in 1566, and English in 1625. Toward the middle of the seventeenth century (1660) came another rather long digest in Balthazar Telles's exceptionally useful *Historia geral da Ethiopia a Alta*, which was issued in an abridged English edition in 1710.

As the preceding view indicates, the Ethiopian version of the Queen of Sheba story was available by the end of the seventeenth century, at least in summary form, in several of the major literary languages of the Western world; but it was not until toward the end of the eighteenth century that the story in the extended Ethiopian form became available in the Christian West.

The primary Ethiopian source of information about the career of Queen Makeda is the *Kebra Nagast* (*Glory of the Kings*) which is the magnum opus of Ethiopian historical traditions and which has long been accorded a degree of reverence in the country matched only by the Bible itself. Owing to the vicissitudes of the past and the difficulty of preserving parchment and vellum manuscripts over long periods in tropical countries with a heavy rainfall, the oldest surviving manuscript of the *Kebra Nagast* is generally said to date no further back than the fourteenth century. It has been supposed, therefore, that this available manuscript is but a copy of an older edition which, in the opinion of some scholars, was written in the sixth century of the Christian era; other authorities would push the date back to the fourth century A.D.

During James Bruce's travels in Ethiopia between 1769 and 1772 he acquired, along with a priceless collection of other manuscripts, two copies of the *Kebra Nagast* which he subsequently gave to the Bodleian Library at Oxford University, where they were studied by August Dillmann, who in 1884 published a description of them in his *Catalogue of Ethiopic MSS in the Bodleian Library*. Five years before Dillmann's *Catalogue* appeared, his countryman, Karl Richard Lepsius, while in Egypt, purchased a manuscript copy of the *Kebra Nagast* from Domingo Lorda which he sent to the Royal Library in Berlin in 1843, and of which a Latin translation was published by Francis Praetorius in 1870. Three years before the latter date, the Napier Expedition, in the course of its campaign in Ethiopia in 1867, captured over nine hundred Ethiopian manuscripts which Ethiopian King Theodore had assembled for the library of his great cathedral being constructed at Magdala. In this collection of manuscripts were two copies of the *Kebra Nagast* that eventually found their way into the British Museum where they were studied by William Wright, who published a description of them and a summary of their contents in 1877.

All of these manuscripts, and others that later reached Europe by various means, were intensively studied, translated, and published in several Western languages. As a consequence of their easy accessibility, these invaluable primary source materials relating to the hitherto little known Ethiopian queen became an increasingly favorite topic in learned and literary circles in the Western world. Poets, novelists, biblical commentators, writers for encyclopedias, and historians were inspired to take to pen and paper by the engaging character of the Ethiopian version of the Sheba story. Some of these efforts were of exceptional merit. In Bruce's *Travels to Discover the Source of the Nile*, first published in 1790, and particularly in the third edition, which appeared in 1813, there were excellent summaries of Queen Makeda's story as it is told in his copies of the *Kebra Nagast*; and to this were added some very revealing comments on the historical authenticity of the account. In 1862 Henry A. Stern, despite his rather skeptical attitude toward some elements in the tradition, presented in his *Wanderings Among the Fala-*

shas some very revealing details about contemporary conditions in Ethiopia that were quite helpful to scholars interested in assaying the historical value of the story. The learned Louis J. Morie in his inclusive, if often thoroughly exasperating, *Histoire de l'Ethiopie*, published in 1904, included the most arresting digest of Queen Makeda's career that had appeared up to that time in any European language. Hard on the heels of this enigmatic publication came H. Le Roux's *Chez la Reine de Saba: Chronique Ethiopienne* which appeared in Paris in 1914.

Sir Wallis Budge, who, paradoxically enough, was at one and the same time Britain's *bon ange* and *bête noire* of Ethiopian studies, was the author of two notable publications. The first of these, published in 1922, bore the arresting title *The Queen of Sheba and Her Only Son Menyelek*, and became the only available full-length English version of that part of the *Kebra Nagast* concerned specifically with Makeda's story. The second of Budge's efforts in this particular connection was his astonishingly learned and most useful, though often thoroughly tendentious, *History of Ethiopia, Nubia, and Abyssinia*, which was published in 1928. Though marred, as is too often true in a number of his writings, by his undisguised bias against black peoples, as well as by a certain looseness which frequently disfigured his prodigious scholarly efforts—these two publications contain, nevertheless, more specific background information about Ethiopia's position in the Queen of Sheba tradition than had ever been assembled by any single author in any language. If used with critical care, they are and will no doubt long remain of unparalleled value to all who are interested in acquiring a detailed acquaintance with the engaging theme with which they are concerned.

The dynasty to which Makeda belonged is estimated, from the traditions available, to have been established in Ethiopia around the year 1370 B.C. Its founder is said to have been Za Besi Angabo who replaced the last representative of an older dynasty known in tradition as the Arwe royal line, and which is generally supposed by modern scholars to have been of foreign origin. The region or country from which this line came is, however, a matter about which tradition is silent; but since it is reported that its representatives were "worshippers of the serpent," it has been suggested that they may have been from Egypt, where the serpent was regarded both as a symbol of wisdom and of royal authority. And there are indeed some cogent bits of evidence which indicate that certain rulers of the great eighteenth dynasty in Egypt, or their vassals, may have ruled over part of Ethiopia during the fifteenth and fourteenth centuries B.C.

The dynasty inaugurated by Za Besi Angabo is thought to have maintained its rule in the country for about 350 years during which period a score or more of monarchs may be presumed to have reigned; but of this number tradition has preserved the names of only a few. The last two of these were Queen Makeda's grandfather and father respectively. The grandfather was Za Sebado who is said to have reigned from about 1076–1026 B.C.; his wife and queen was named Ceres. They had an only child, a daughter who married Za Sebado's chief minister. When Za Sebado died this son-in-law became the country's king in his stead, and reigned from about 1026–1005 B.C. To him and his wife, Queen Ismenie, were born two children; first, a son, Prince Noural Rouz, whose name meant "the light of day"; and second, a daughter, Princess Makeda, who is said to have been born in 1020 B.C. While Prince Noural was still an infant his nurse accidentally let him fall into the fire which caused his death; and later, Princess Makeda, while also a child, is said by tradition to have been attacked by a pet jackal which bit her rather badly on one foot and leg, leaving some lasting scars which, fortunately, did not affect her walk. The injury received at the time of this incident is supposed to have been responsible for a later Moslem tradition to the effect that one of the Queen's limbs was deformed and resembled that of an ass.

When her father died in about the year 1005 B.C., Makeda, being his only heir, ascended the throne and reigned until about the year 955 B.C. The young queen is said by tradition to have been "very beautiful in face; her stature was superb and her understanding and intelligence were very great." It is further reported that she was "exceedingly rich, for God had given her glory and riches and gold and silver and splendid apparel and camels and slaves and caravans which trafficked for her by sea and by land from India to Syene" (Egypt's great southern market town known in later time as Aswan).

Among the great merchant princes of Ethiopia at that time was one Tamrin who is reported to have owned almost four hundred ships and caravans numbering over five hundred camels which he employed in his extensive commercial operations. Among his customers were King Solomon of Jerusalem to whom Tamrin went on one occasion to deliver a large order of Ethiopia's natural products, including red gold, sapphires, and black wood that could not be bored by worms (ebony). During his sojourn in Jerusalem on this occasion Tamrin greatly admired the wisdom of Solomon, and the manner in which he ruled his people and administered his kingdom. The merchant prince also was deeply impressed by the Hebrew king's direct and fluent speech. We are told as well that Tamrin was amazed at Solomon's impartiality, justice, and the great wealth and splendor in which he lived.

On his return to Ethiopia, the merchant prince gave his queen a glowing and detailed account of all the marvels which he had witnessed during his sojourn in Jerusalem. Special emphasis was placed upon the wisdom and the other extraordinary natural endowments of the Hebrew king. The more the queen heard, the more she marveled and desired to go to Jerusalem in order to meet Solomon and learn from him. Having disclosed to her people her desires in this respect and having received their approval, Makeda named Tamrin the captain and chief of the caravan by which she intended to travel to Jerusalem and ordered him to make all preparations necessary for the journey. When the caravan, which consisted of about eight hundred camels and countless mules and asses, was ready, Queen Makeda, along with many attendants, set out on her journey with great pomp and majesty and an enormous baggage train.

When she arrived in Jerusalem, Solomon welcomed her cordially, paid her great honors, and gave her apartments in his palace. His cooks supplied her and the members of her party with food both morning and evening and sent her wine, honey, and sweetmeats from his own table. From time to time, Solomon visited with the queen and took great delight in her company and conversation and she, in turn, was equally delighted with the courtesy of the king's behavior toward her and by his wisdom and his judgment. In the many long and frequent conversations that took place between the maiden queen and her gracious host, several questions about many matters were mutually asked and answered. Religion was one of the principal topics which often claimed their attention, and when Solomon explained to the queen the might and power of the "one true God, the God of Israel," she was convinced. She allegedly abandoned the worship of the sun and became a follower of the God of Israel.

After Makeda had spent six months in Jerusalem under such pleasant and profitable circumstances, she informed King Solomon that while she would like very much to remain in his capital, and continue under his tutelage in order to grow in wisdom and in the knowledge of the religion of Israel, the time had come when duty required that she return to her own land. This distressed Solomon very much. He was most reluctant to part with his gracious and lovely visitor, and pondered the matter of marrying her. With this in mind, the king pled with the queen not to leave him in haste but to prolong her sojourn for yet another season in order that he might "complete her instructions in wisdom." Queen Makeda, in her innocence, accepted this invitation at its face value, but in due course discovered that Solomon's intentions were not altogether quite as honorable as she had come to suppose, for, despite his wisdom, Solomon was, in the words of Holy Writ, "one whose heart was not perfect with the Lord." The virgin queen tried as best she could to safeguard her virginity, but her strivings in the end proved of no avail against the "wayward wiles of the wisest of wayward men."*

Some months after this unexpected and novel experience, Makeda said to Solomon, "Dismiss me, and let me depart to my own country," and the king after giving her many rich presents, including a ring for whom he hoped would be their son, said: "Go in peace and may the peace of God go with thee." When she arrived at a village on the outskirts of her kingdom the pains of childbirth seized her and she brought forth a man-child whom she named Ebna Hakim, meaning "son of the wise man."

Although Queen Makeda seems to have maintained a residence at or in the vicinity of Axum, situated in the beautiful and cool highlands in the northern part of the kingdom, the main seat of the government (or her capital city) appears to have been on or near the coast towards the southern end of the African shore of the Red Sea, and in a district, the name of which is variously remembered as Azab or

---

* Following one of those dinners at which highly seasoned meats were featured, so one version of the legend goes, Solomon invited the queen to spend the night in his quarters. She agreed to do so on condition that he not violate her person; Solomon accepted that on condition that she not take anything of his. Having thus reached an agreement, the two retired for the night. During the night the queen awoke and took a drink of water, only to find that Solomon had expected this. He thus justified taking her to his bed because she had broken the agreement.

Asabe or Saba, which meant in the Ethiopian languages of the time "the southern lands" or "the lands of the south." The name "Sheba," it has been widely supposed, was either a variation of the same name, or a specific designation of a part of the same district or neighboring region. In the course of time the specific seat of the government or the capital city itself would seem to have been known by the same name or names.

It is of interest to note in passing that there is in this southern region . . . a seaport town which is known as Assab, and that James Bruce, writing nearly two hundred years ago, reported that at a short distance to the back of this town there were still to be seen impressive ruins representing what were obviously the remains of splendid buildings that had once stood on that site. Here it is also worthy of noting that, in 1939, the veteran Austrian explorer, Byron de Prorok Kühn, discovered in an arid and uninhabitable region in French Somaliland (now known as Afars and Issas), less than one hundred miles further south, a remarkable aggregation of ruined buildings and ancient tombs which he tentatively dated to the age in which the Queen of Sheba had lived. In the light of this evidence, it is not too much to say that the ancient ruins which have been reported by Bruce and de Prorok Kühn may well be relics of the civilization which flourished in the Azab or Asabe district when Queen Makeda and the members of her royal house were lords of "the Lands in the South."

But whether or not these suggestions are in accord with what were the historical facts, it is true that the *Kebra Nagast* tells us that after Makeda returned to Asab, her kingdom continued to wax in riches and renown under her able rule and that with the passing of the years, her son, Ebna Hakim, grew in stature and strength and became more like his famous father every day. When the prince was twenty-two years of age, his mother, in keeping with her promise to Solomon just before leaving Jerusalem, sent him to visit his father under the care of the faithful and now aging Tamrin, who was her chief Minister of State. Solomon, as were his people at large, was overjoyed to see his handsome and noble-minded son; for what a contrast he was to Solomon's only other male heir, Rheabom, of whom it was written that he was "ample in foolishness and lacking in understanding." For this reason, Solomon did his best to persuade Ebna Hakim to remain in Jerusalem, with the intention of making him his successor; but the young prince was deaf to his father's pleas, and insisted on returning to "the mountains of mother's land." Being finally convinced that his son was determined to have his own way in this matter, Solomon commanded that everything be made ready for the return journey.

Shortly after the prince arrived in Jerusalem he had disclosed to his father Queen Makeda's wish to extend in her country the growth and development of the religion of Israel. Solomon, in keeping with this information, decided to send a number of Hebrews, learned in the Law, back to Ethiopia with his son to aid in proselytizing. With this end in mind, Solomon commanded his counselors to select and dedicate one each of their sons to this noble purpose. In response, the counselors prepared their eldest sons for the journey to Ethiopia; but even though they pretended to Solomon that they were obeying with good will, they cursed him for robbing them of their sons. Nor were the sons themselves altogether happy over their new prospects. For in going to Ethiopia, so they believed, they no longer would be under the protection which their God Jehovah had promised their ancestors in the days of Moses. Azarias, the son of the High Priest Zadak, and one of the young men who had been chosen to go to Ethiopia, had a bright idea: why not take with them to Ethiopia the ark containing the covenant and the other holy relics? In discusing the matter with those who were to be his companions, all agreed that this must be done; but the plan would have to be a jealously guarded secret to which not even the prince should be a party.

Some months later when all preparations for the journey had been completed and Solomon had provided his son with rich presents and bade him a sad farewell, Azarias and his companions, on the night before the morning of the grand departure, removed the ark containing the covenant from its accustomed place, and substituted for it a chest of the same size and shape. After carefully covering this with the mantle customarily employed for protecting the holy relic from the dust, Azarias and his companions hid the ark with the covenant in one of the wagons containing their baggage; and on the next morning headed with it for their new home in far off Ethiopia. Several days later when the High Priest Zadak discovered what had been done, he and King Solomon ordered swift horsemen to overtake the departed caravan, repossess the holy relics, and bring them back to Jerusalem; but according to tradition, God himself confounded the pursuers by miraculously sweeping the whole caravan forward with such swiftness that it was never overtaken. Azarias and his companions thus remained in possession of their holy treasure; and the whole caravan, with Tamrin and Prince Ebna Hakim at its head, arrived in due course, safe and sound, at its intended destination. Thus, says tradition, were the ark and the covenant transported from the Land of Israel to the Kingdom of Ethiopia.

Unfortunately, we learn from neither the *Kebra Nagast* nor from any of the other surviving traditions anything about how Queen Makeda and her son felt when they heard what Azarias and his companions had done. There is every indication that the young émigrés were very proud of their achievement, and it well may be that the Queen and her son accepted the *fait accompli* as an act of destiny. At any rate, tradition clearly indicates that Azarias and his companions settled down quite contentedly in their new homeland and, with royal support, pursued quite successfully the missionary task to which they had been called. Having taken unto themselves wives from among the people of the country, they founded families of their own and brought up their progeny in accordance with the ancient Hebrew Law. The offspring of their converts were trained in the same way. Thus was established in the country, according to various national traditions, those who came to be known as the *Falashas* ("Black Jews") who have formed a significant part of the Ethiopian population from ancient times down to our own day.

Queen Makeda, according to tradition, lived for a number of years after her son's return from Jerusalem, and when she died around 955 B.C., she was succeeded by Ebna Hakim who, on his ascendency, took the throne name Menelik I. Tradition reports that the Queen was buried, not at Azab in the south, but at Axum in the north; and in the course of Menelik's reign, this city was also made the chief seat of the government. Why the king took the latter step is not indicated in the surviving traditions but it may be surmised that two considerations prompted the change. In the first place, Axum, owing to its great altitude, enjoyed a decidedly more genial climate than did lowland Asab; and in the second place, it is quite probable that Menelik and others revered the city since Makeda was buried there; the change thus enabled the king to visit more often his mother's tomb.

Here then is an account of the Ethiopian version of the career of Queen Makeda, who, the Ethiopians are quite convinced, is to be identified with the biblical Queen of Sheba. One of the principal pieces of external evidence in support of this contention is the reference in the New Testament in which Solomon's famous royal visitor is specifically called the "Queen of the South." In this connection it is pointed out that in the *Book of Axum*, which is second only to the *Kebra Nagast* as a source of authoritative Ethiopian traditions, and which is written in ancient Ge'ez or Ethiopic, that Makeda's capital was in the "district of Azeba," meaning, as already pointed out, "Country of the South." And again in the New Testament there are passages in which Solomon's visitor is mentioned as: "Queen of the South," which is rendered in the Tigrinya language as *Eteye Azeb*— "Ruler of the South."

The second bit of external testimony which lends support to the Ethiopian version of the legend is the fact that all of the products which are named in the Old Testament texts as having been carried by the Queen of Sheba as gifts to Solomon—stores of spices, gold, and precious stones—were all not only native to Makeda's kingdom but, in comparison with neighboring countries, abundant there. Within her own domain there were the rich gold fields in the Fazoli region, and, as ancient workings have revealed, in the Keren district in the north and the Edola area in the south. In the nearby kingdoms of Kush there were prolific gold fields; and hardly less rich were the old Nilotic gold fields lying between the second and third cataracts. The historical and archaeological evidence suggests that it was from these ancient Ethiopian gold-producing regions, along with the gold trade of distant Sofala, that the classical civilizations of the ancient occidental world derived the greater part of their gold supplies. Ethiopia indeed had access to an abundance of gold.

As for precious stones, the famed emerald mines in the lower Nubian Desert east of the Nile would appear to have been second to none; and the harvests of pearls from some of Ethiopia's Red Sea isles would appear to have been beyond compare. Sapphires were also plentiful and the "topazes of Ethiopia" were then of proverbial renown. The "blessed land of Punt" which was the ancient Egyptian designation for Queen Makeda's ancestral domain, had been famous for the varieties and abundance of its spice plants ever since history began; nor is it to be overlooked that the "ebony, ivory, and apes" which Solomon sought—and which may well have been among Makeda's presents—were found in great plenty in those parts. Thus, the Queen of Sheba's reported gifts to King Solomon of "much gold and precious stones and a great store of spices" could well have been acquired by Queen Makeda without any particular difficulty.

This leaves for consideration the view that the biblical Queen of Sheba was an ancient Arabian princess named Belkis, and that the Yemenite kingdom of Saba or Himyar was her ancient domain. Most of the traditions to this effect are of rabbinical and Arabic origin and date, for the most part, from the Middle Ages. It was not, however, until well into modern times that these traditions were made conveniently accessible to scholars at large in the Western world. A few fragments of these traditions were contained in Bartolocci's famous collection of rabbinical traditions which was published in Rome under the title *Bibliotheca Magna Rabbinica* between 1675 and 1693. This was followed by Eisenmenger's *Neu-en-dektes Judenthum* which was published in Königsberg in 1711.

Among the Arabs, the earliest traditional reference relating to the Queen of Sheba is a curious passage in Chapter Twenty-seven of the Koran in which the Prophet Mohammed refers to correspondence and relationships between King Solomon and the "Queen of Saba"—communications and relationships which do not present the Hebrew king in a favorable light. Of particular importance are the *Annals* of the great Arab traditionalist and historian, Mohammed Al Tabari (838–923 A.D.) who tells the story of Belkis's relationship with King Solomon at considerable length, but with what has been described as "so much gorgeous embellishment as to resemble a fairy tale rather than an episode in a serious narrative."

Of special interest among the works of Arabic authors was an unpublished manuscript by the Moslem writer Hamdani who died in the city of Sana about the middle of the tenth century, but whose manuscript was unknown in the West until discovered by Commander Craufurd in Arabia in the nineteenth century. What gives this particular document its special interest is the fact that Hamdani states that

Belkis was the daughter of the king of Yemen and an Ethiopian princess named Ekeye Azeb. According to this author, Belkis was born in Mareb, then the capital of the Sabaean or Yemenite empire. She is said to have spent her youth in Ethiopia but returned to Mareb just before her father's death; and following that event, she is reported to have been elected by the people as the first woman to rule over the empire.

Notable among other Moslem authors whose writings refer to Belkis's relationship with Solomon, special mention should be made of Nuvaire (d. 1340), who says she was the sixteenth successor of Himyar, the founder of the Himyarite dynasty in Yemen, and who dates the beginning of her reign circa 991 B.C. There are also the traditionalists Al Beidawi and Jallalod'din whose fabulous tales of Belkis's relationships with Solomon are hardly less mythical in character than are the fanciful outpourings of the great Tabari. In the same category must be placed the collected traditions of Ibn al Hasan Addiar Bekri, Alabi din Al Bakri, and Mohammed Ibn Ahmed Alakissai. These were first made available to Western scholars, unacquainted with Arabic, through Gustav Weil's notable *Biblische Legenden der Muselmanner*, published in Frankfurt in 1845. Weil's valuable volume was followed by Herman Zolenberg's translation and publication of Tabari's chronicle which appeared in Paris in 1867.

The Prophet Mohammed's allusions to the Queen of Saba or Sheba were first made available in the West in a non-oriental language when the Koran was translated into Latin by Peter the Venerable, Abbot of Cluny, around 1141; and knowledge of the passage was widened with a translation in English which appeared in London in 1649. Then came George Sale's famous English translation of the Koran which appeared in 1734, and to which he attached, in the form of notes, a number of extracts from the collected traditions of Al Beidawi and Jallalod'din.

Borrowing and adopting a remark which William F. Albright once expressed in a related connection, most Arabic versions of the Sheba story betray their character as fiction not only by their all too frequent vagueness and conflicting traditions about historical and geographical detail, but also by their *mise en scène* which is either mythical or improbable. Let us examine a few reported episodes which are typical of the whole story and which would seem to bear out the validity of Albright's comments.

Hamdani, as we have seen, says that Belkis was the daughter of the Yemenite king, Shar Habil (or Sharhabil), and an Ethiopian princess named Ekeye Azeb; but according to Nuvaire and Abulfeda, she was the daughter of Shar Habil's successor Hadid. Another tradition maintains that Belkis's father was the vizier or prime minister of King Shar Habil, an alleged tyrant, and that her mother was a jinni (a supernatural being that could take human or animal form and influence human affairs). Belkis was born to the vizier and his superhuman wife on an island in the midst of the ocean, to which they were transported for that purpose by magic. According to tradition, on their return to Arabia and after Belkis was grown up, King Shar Habil asked for the hand of the exceptionally beautiful daughter of the prime minister. Before the marriage was consummated, Belkis got her spouse drunk and cut off his head. When she announced to the assembled multitude what she had done, there were shouts of joy and Belkis was straightaway elected ruler of the kingdom.

For the next twenty years Belkis ruled the kingdom of Himyar with the heart of a woman but with the head and hand of a man, and Yemen flourished like the proverbial green tree. Then a strange and very shocking thing happened. One day while Belkis was in her boudoir with all doors closed, a bird flew in through an open window and dropped a letter in her lap.

On opening the letter, the startled queen read:

Greetings from Solomon, Son of David, and servant of the Most High God to Belkis, Queen of Saba. You are aware that God has made me lord and king over the wild beasts and the birds of heaven and over the devils and spirits and ghosts of the night. You are aware, moreover, that God has made me great lord over all kings from the lands of the rising to the land of the setting sun. . . . Rise, therefore, not up against me but come and surrender yourself unto me. Do as I bid and no harm, but much honor, will be yours. . . . But if you disobey my command and try to resist me, I shall send against you my armies of ghosts, and devils which will slay you in your bed at night; and my armies of birds and wild beasts will tear your flesh and chew your bones.

Having read the letter to her councilors and sought their advice on how she should react to it, it was finally decided to send an ambassador with a curious assortment of presents to Solomon, both for the purpose of testing his alleged superhuman powers and of placating him if possible. The presents included among other things a thousand carpets woven of gold and silver tissue; five hundred bricks of gold; five hundred girls dressed as boys; five hundred boys dressed as girls; and a crystal goblet which Solomon was to be asked to fill with water which came "neither from earth or heaven." If Solomon was the all-knowing and all-powerful man he claimed himself to be, he would have no trouble distinguishing the girls from the boys despite their dress; nor would the filling of the goblet be a problem. And it was agreed that if Solomon could do these things he was indeed a great wizard and it would be wise for all Saba to submit to him.

But where was the embassy to find this self-acclaimed wizard of a king? That was the question. The morning of the day he dispatched his letter, he was in Mecca, but by noon he was in Sana over four hundred miles farther south—for according to Jallalod'din, Solomon had a mighty magic carpet, made of green silk, on which he and all of his armies, as well as his mighty throne, were transported at the king's command through the air with lightening-like speed by the wind. Having reached Sana in this miraculous manner, Solomon discovered that there was not enough water in the city for him to take a bath, so he ordered his little lapwing—the same which had delivered his letter—to scout the country for a well. While winging her way over the desert in keeping with Solomon's command, the lapwing sighted the city of Saba with all of its riches, and the beautiful Belkis, its beloved queen; and on returning to Solomon the lapwing reported to the king on all that she had seen. This glowing account moved the mighty monarch to dispatch his letter by the faithful little lapwing to Belkis, ordering her to surrender herself and her city to him.

When the members of the mission which Belkis had decided to send to Solomon were all ready to start, but at a loss about how and where to reach the king, the omniscient and omnipotent potentate speedily resolved their problem without even being asked. Solomon had his jinn roll out the magic carpet to the point where the members of the embassy were standing and wondering about the direction in which to turn their steps. Having walked unwittingly on to the magic carpet they were astonished to find themselves a moment later standing in the presence of Solomon, arrayed in all his glory and seated on his mighty throne. When the presents which were intended to mystify the monarch were presented to him, he unraveled each riddle without one "whit" of difficulty.

When the embassy returned to Saba and reported in detail all that had happened, Belkis, in keeping with her promise to herself, set out at once for Solomon's camp. She was now convinced that there was nothing she could do but capitulate to this wonderworking potentate. Thus, when she and her army of twelve thousand men were only a few miles away, Solomon decided to confront Saba's queen with a great surprise. He ordered his chief jinni to fetch Belkis's throne, then in her capital several hundred miles away, and place it beside his own. When the great demon promised that the task would be done by noon, Solomon replied that that would be too late, for the queen would be arriving very soon. Whereupon Asaph, Solomon's wonderworking vizier, promised that he would have the throne transported instantly and he was as good as his word; for there the throne stood on the magic carpet beside Solomon's own, and all in less time than it took the king to bat an eye!

When the news arrived that Belkis the Beautiful was on her way to Solomon's portable court, some of his jinn—or more likely some of his many wives and girl friends—developed a violent jealousy toward her even before she arrived. They told the king that they had heard on reliable authority that though Belkis was beautiful above the waist in both body and face, her lower extremities left much to be desired. According to Tabari's account she had very hairy legs. According to another Arab version her legs resembled exactly "those of an ass." Her deformity had been brought about, so the rumor ran, when her father, while she was yet a child, had killed a giant serpent and some of its blood had spewed on what were then the little princess's pretty legs and feet. To hide her disfigurement, so tradition avowed, she had ever since worn long robes to shield her unsightly underpinnings from public view.

Solomon decided not to accept these rumors about the queen's physical handicaps without finding out the facts for himself. With this in mind, Solomon ordered his jinn to lay down a pavement of crystal, covered with a thin coating of water, directly in front of the place where his own and the queen's throne stood. This was then sprinkled with rose petals so that the ruse could not be too quickly discerned. And sure enough when Belkis appeared she was wearing a long robe which hid her legs from the eyes of men and women alike. But Solomon, thanks to his crystal pavement disguised to look like water, was quite certain that he would succeed in finding out what he now wished most to know. At the presentation ceremony, while Belkis was walking in a stately manner toward Solomon, she caught sight of what appeared to be her own throne. Distracted by this great surprise, she stepped onto the crystal pavements before she was quite aware of what she was doing. On suddenly looking down she observed that she was about to step into what appeared to be deep water, and to keep her robe from getting wet, she instinctively lifted it to her knees; and Solomon saw what he most wished to see—the beautiful Belkis's legs and feet were normal in every respect except one, on one leg there were three unsightly goat hairs!

Notwithstanding this blemish, Solomon fell deeply in love with Saba's queen and wished to marry her. The three goat hairs on the queen's leg caused him, however, to hesitate. Then with the aid of one of his jinn, assisted by the devil, he concocted a preparation by which the unsightly goat hairs were removed—this was, so we are informed, the first depilatory in human history.

There was now no longer any reason to hesitate, so Solomon made Belkis his wife and converted her from sun-worship to the worship of the one true God. She gave the whole of her realm to her husband but he returned it to her, and she later resumed there her customary rule. When returning to her own kingdom she carried with her "the fruit of her union with Solomon," and not too long after that she bore a son who subsequently became, so Tabari and others inform us, "the ancestor of the Ethiopian kings."

When Belkis died, Solomon, so tradition avows, had her body conveyed to Tadmor, a desert city which she had built; but where she was entombed was eventually forgotten, and the place remained unknown, says tradition, until the eighth century of the Christian era. During the reign of Caliph Walid I (705–715), or Caliph Walid II (743–744), a heavy cloudburst caused many walls in the town of Tadmor to collapse, revealing in a certain place, according to one account, "an iron sarcophagus which was sixty ells long and forty ells wide." On the sarcophagus was an inscription which read:

> Here lies the pious Belkis, Queen of Sheba, wife of the Prophet Solomon, Son of David. She was converted to the true faith in the thirteenth year of the reign of Solomon; she married him in the fourteenth and died in the three and twentieth year of his reign.

By the order of Caliph Walid the sarcophagus was left where it was found and a mausoleum, built of marble, was erected over it so that "it might not again be disturbed by the hand of man."

Thus are reviewed the pre-eminent biblical, Ethiopian, Arabic, and rabbinical accounts of the fabled but enticingly mysterious Queen of Sheba. Which of them bears the greatest core of truth? Certainly there are enough similar strains in the various traditions for almost all of the sources to hold themselves up as "the one true story," although the embellishments and anthropomorphic additions in some of the latter writings almost cast them into the realm of fantasy.

A critical and balanced weighing of the evidence, however, lends the most nearly conclusive support to the Ethiopian claim of having been the homeland of the famed "Queen of the South." The character of the natural resources and the history of commercial enterprises and operations in Ethiopia in ancient times most assuredly dovetail with corresponding details in the Ethiopian legends. Archaeological discoveries—such as the site of the city of Axum, its venerated churches, and the mausoleum of Menelik I—buttress claims of the high character of the material civilization of this nation in antiquity and provide additional internal evidence supporting some of the facts mentioned in that country's various historical tracts.

Finally, the confluence of certain basic elements in the tomes of such respected authors and antiquarians as Flavius Josephus, Abu Salih, Pedro Paez, and Balthazar Telles—as well as a number of distinguished modern scholars such as James Bruce, Louis J. Morie and J. L. Krapf—undergird the Ethiopian version on this royal "seeker of wisdom" in such a manner as to leave little doubt as to the validity of the long-established claim of the world's second oldest Christian kingdom to being the motherland of one of history's most regal figures—the Queen of Sheba, the source of the ruling dynasty of Ethiopia.

II

Ezana the Great and the Emergence of Ethiopia as a Christian State

The roots of Ethiopian history may be traced to the Kingdom of Axum, which emerged sometime during the pre-Christian millenium and became the dominant kingdom in northeastern Africa during the fourth century A.D. By the latter date, Axum had developed a viable political state which practiced an advanced agriculture, engaged in a vigorous trade with other Africans and inhabitants of the Middle East, produced highly skilled architects and builders in stone, and maintained a victorious army equipped with iron weapons, a phenomenon for many ancient peoples. The most famous ruler of Axum during this flourishing era was the fourth-century emperor, Ezana, who is credited with making Christianity the official religion of his kingdom, an event destined to influence the whole structure of Ethiopian society. This highly significant achievement apparently occurred around 330 A.D., although in none of his remaining inscriptions did Ezana mention it.

Not only is Ezana's reign important because of the establishment of official Christianity, it is also significant be-

cause of the historical light it sheds on Axum and neighboring areas for which we have few other sources of information. The Axumites left to posterity several stone-cut inscriptions in Sabaean (the language of the early settlers of Axum), Ge'ez (Ethiopic, the language evolved by the Axumites themselves), and Greek (in which the early rulers of Axum were well-versed). Several of those inscriptions recount the affairs of state and war during Ezana's regime. One of them describes his defeat of neighboring Meroë, that great Nile River polity of ancient times, and thus provides a date (350 A.D.) which many authorities believe marks the end of the state of Meroë. Another inscription cites a number of old cities and towns no longer existent, but which thrived in ancient times.

The historical significance of Ezana and his regime is therefore obvious; and the following essay by Professor Hansberry presents an evaluative account of the great ancient Ethiopian ruler.

The Editor

Ezana was probably born around 310 A.D. and died around 356 A.D. His father was the Axumite King Ella Amida, who reigned from approximately 294 to 325 A.D. When King Ella Amida died in 325, Ezana and his brother, Asbeha, were minors; thus their mother became the queen regent and ruled the country in this capacity from about 325 to 328. At that time Ezana (also known as Abreha) and his brother were old enough to govern the country jointly in their own names.

According to this chronology, Ella Amida had a comparatively long reign, but unfortunately tradition has preserved very few particulars about the history of the country during this period. According to Eusebius of Caesarea, ambassadors from Ethiopia visited the Roman Empire in Constantine's reign for the purpose of congratulating him on his victory over the Goths and on the peace and prosperity which then prevailed in his empire. Exactly when this Ethiopian embassy arrived is unknown, but if the tradition is founded upon historical facts, the event must have occurred either in Ella Amida's reign or during the regency of his queen. Another event of epoch-making significance also occurred during this same period. This was the first of a series of events which eventually culminated in the emergence of Ethiopia as a Christian state. However, before examining those developments, it is appropriate first to consider the Christian influence in Axum prior to its official recognition.

Exactly when and how Christianity first appeared in Ethiopia are questions which cannot be answered with any certainty. The earliest and best known of all traditions associated with the area is the well-known and most engaging passage which appears in the New Testament: The Acts, Chapter Eight, verses twenty-six through thirty-nine. There it is recorded that the apostle Philip while traveling the road from Jerusalem to Gaza met "a man of Ethiopia" who had been to worship in Jerusalem, and who was of "great authority [as treasurer] under Candace, queen of the Ethiopians."

Philip, so the story goes, joined himself to the chariot of the Ethiopian, and observed that the Ethiopian was reading from the Prophet Isaiah, and Philip asked: "Understandest thou what thou readest?" The Ethiopian replied: "How can I, except some man should guide me?" Philip thus discussed the passages with the Ethiopian and "preached unto him Jesus." Later, the Ethiopian on seeing a body of water said to Philip: ". . . what doth hinder me to be baptized?" And Philip replied: "If thou believest with all thine heart, thou mayest." When the Ethiopian said he believed in Jesus, the two men stopped near the water, where Philip baptized the Ethiopian; they then went their separate ways. Many Ethiopians believe that this treasurer of Candace was the first to preach in Ethiopia.

Since the term "Ethiopia" was a rather inclusive, yet an indefinite, one known to the classical writers as including all those areas to the south and southeast of Egypt, it is impossible to say whether this reference in The Acts related to the more limited regions known today as Ethiopia, or to the neighboring region of Meroë. A number of scholars, basing their position upon the fact that the term *Candace* is known to have been the title of a Queen Mother of Meroë who fought the Romans of Augustus Caesar, are disposed to think that the personages mentioned in the biblical text were Nubians rather than inhabitants of the Ethiopian kingdom of Axum. This view is, however, by no means shared by the Ethiopians themselves, for their traditions clearly indicate that the queen mentioned in the passage was beyond all question a member of the Ethiopian royal family.

The biblical account gives neither the name of the "man of Ethiopia," nor the results of the newly converted official's religious efforts in Ethiopia. According to one Ethiopian account, Philip's convert was a Jew named Djan Darada who is said to have been the chamberlain or chief steward of Queen Garsemot IV of the ancient kingdom of Axum. In another surviving tradition, however, the chamberlain is said to have been an Ethiopian nobleman named Juda, who was Jewish, and the queen, who is said to have been the regent of Axum, named Judith. In both of these versions it is reported that on his return to Axum the chamberlain succeeded in converting the queen. In commemoration of her conversion, so one Ethiopian tradition relates, the queen dedicated an ancient temple, allegedly built by the Queen of Sheba, to the service of the new religion. According to another tradition, however, the queen caused a great church to be built in her capital city and the cornerstone for this church is reported to have been sent to the queen from Jerusalem by the Apostles themselves.

Although the record is not as complete as could be desired, a number of accounts are available which give a clearer picture of the main outline of the historical circumstances under which Christianity came to be established as the official or state religion of the Axumite empire. The longest and the best known and most often quoted of the non-Ethiopian accounts is that by the noted church historian, Rufinus of Tyre (350–410 A.D.). But similar accounts have come down to us in the writings of the church historians Socrates and Sozemius, both of whom were, like Rufinus, more or less contemporary with the events which they recorded. There are also other brief and scattered refrences to the same series of events in the writings of certain other classical authors, dating from the same general period. Although these accounts differ here and there in matters of detail, the main outline of the story recorded in each is in substantial agreement. The story, as it is recorded in these classical sources, parallels rather closely what Ethiopian tradition reports concerning the circumstances under which Christianity came to be permanently established in the country.

Early in the fourth century of the Christian Era, Metrodore, who is said to have been a philosopher living in the city of Tyre, is reported to have visited among other lands the countries of Persia, India, and Ethiopia. In the course of his travels he reportedly acquired a considerable collection of large pearls and rare and valuable precious stones. A part of his collection is said to have been taken by the king of Persia, and it is reported that he subsequently sold or gave some of the best of his pearls and gems to the Roman Emperor Constantine. On his return to Tyre, Metrodore related in some detail to a fellow townsman the observations and experiences he had incurred during his travels. This townsman, named Meropius, is described as having been both a philosopher and a merchant prince. So impressed was Meropius with Metrodore's account that he resolved to undertake a similar journey himself.

In due course, Meropius set out for the east, accompanied by two young companions, one of whom was named Frumentius and the other Edesius. According to some accounts, the two young men were his nephews; other accounts declare that they were his sons and students. While sailing through the Red Sea, the ship on which they were traveling is said by one account to have been wrecked on the rocks and all persons on board except the two youths, Frumentius and Edesius, are reported to have drowned or to have died of injuries or exposure. Another and more generally accepted version of this story holds that the ship on which the seafarers were traveling put in at an Ethiopian port for the purpose of obtaining food and water supplies.

Although the ship's crew had no knowledge of the fact, relationships at that moment were very strained between the inhabitants of the port and Roman or Byzantine vessels sailing in nearby Ethiopian waters. Sometime before Meropius's ship put into the Ethiopian port, the place had been visited by a Greek trading vessel and a fight had broken out between the ship's crew and some of the inhabitants of the town, and a number of the latter had been injured, or otherwise provoked. As a consequence, the inhabitants not only had broken off trading relationships with Greco-Roman merchants, but vowed vengeance on all who could be identified as countrymen of those who had so recently violated the port's hospitality. Thus, when the Greco-Roman ship on which Meropius and his two young companions were traveling endeavored to tie up at the wharf, the people of the port fell upon the ship's crew and passengers with such fury and suddenness that they were taken wholly by surprise and were quite unable to defend themselves. As a consequence, Meropius and all who were with him were massacred, except Frumentius and Edesius who were taken alive and saved from death because of their youth.

Eventually, the two young men were carried to Axum where they were presented to Ella Amida, who ordered that they be treated with kindness and given living quarters at the court. Before long, they had won completely the king's confidence and esteem, so much so that Edesius was appointed as one of the king's royal cupbearers, while Frumentius, because of his knowledge of Greek, was made one of the king's private secretaries. According to one account, the two young foreigners were closely associated during this period with the king's own sons.

Although the vast majority of the people during this period were adherents of the ancient and traditional religions of the land, there was nonetheless a considerable number of Christians in the country at this time. One of the Ethiopian sources states in this connection that Frumentius and Edesius, both of whom were Christians, "wondered much at the peoples of Ethiopia when they saw so many of them praying to the Blessed Trinity and their women wearing the sign of the cross on their heads." They were curious about how the Ethiopians had come to believe in the faith of Christ when it seemed there had been no apostle and no preaching of this religion among them.

From other independent sources, it is known that Ethiopia, like Nubia, had served for many generations as a refuge for the Egyptian, Syrian, and other Levantine Christians who had been forced to flee from various parts of the Roman empire in order to escape persecutions imposed on them, from time to time, by imperial decrees. And it is also known that numbers of Christians had entered both countries from the Egyptian north and the Middle East for many decades for commercial purposes.*

The Christians whom Frumentius and Edesius saw in Ethiopia were probably émigrés and their descendants who had entered the country under such circumstances. Among the number were also, no doubt, numerous Ethiopians who had been converted to the Christian religion through the ministrations of the emigrants. The available sources suggest that no proscriptions were imposed on proselyting activities by the foreigners and their converts during this period. After some years in the country in this atmosphere, Frumentius and Edesius were informed by Ella Amida, just before his death in 325, that they were at liberty to return to their homeland whenever they pleased. Following the king's death, however, his wife, now queen regent, urged the two young men to remain in the country as her assistants in the government and as members of the tutorial staff in charge of the education of her two sons who were to be the eventual rulers of the land. This invitation was accepted and the new arrangement continued, apparently for a period of about three years. During this time Frumentius and Edesius applied themselves with diligence, but with discretion, to the promotion of Christianity throughout the country. Frumentius is said to have paid special attention to providing places

---

* True or not, many Ethiopians believe the two preceding traditions. In addition, it is important to know that Christian merchants from many foreign lands frequented the principal entrepôts of Ethiopia. In cities like Adulis and Axum, for example, they were not only tolerated as Christians, but were permitted to build their own prayer houses. There is little doubt that many Ethiopians were familiar with Christian ideas and practices and some had converted long before the official recognition of Christianity by Ezana.

for Christian worship and to securing permission for Greek travelers to exercise their religion while sojourning in the land.

The two sons designated by the late king as his heirs were enthroned as co-sovereigns of the country in the year 328. After their coronation, Abreha took the throne name Ezana and his brother Asbeha chose Shaiazana as his throne name. To the nation at large, however, these two princes continued to be known generally as Abreha and Asbeha, and the same practice was followed by all subsequent generations down to our own day. In most of the Ethiopian annals, chronicles, and king lists, the use of the pre-coronation names is limited almost entirely to stone inscriptions dating from their own day. Since it is in the main from these contemporary inscriptions on stone that we have received most of the detailed information concerning the careers and accomplishments of these two royal brothers, modern scholars have shown, on the whole, a preference for the throne name of the two kings when narrating the chief events of their reigns.

Despite their joint tenancy of the imperial throne, Ethiopian traditions record that relationships between the two brothers were remarkably peaceful in every respect and an Ethiopian poet of many centuries ago summed up the situation quite effectively when he wrote:

Peace be to Abreha and Asbeha
They in one kingdom did the scepter sway;
And yet in love and yet in accord still
They lived as princes with one heart and will.

But as peaceful as the dual reign of these two brothers may have been, their roles were by no means equal so far as influence, achievement, and renown were concerned. Ezana was by far the abler and more eminent of the royal pair. Except for an occasional and incidental reference to the younger brother, modern historians have tended to write of this theoretical dual reign as if Ezana alone had been the king during that period. Before reviewing the specific achievements of these two kings, it is appropriate to return briefly to the story of the two Tyrian brothers whose visit to Ethiopia turned out to be an event of epochal significance in the history of the ancient land.

Of these two brothers' subsequent years the career of Frumentius was decidedly the more engaging and pertinent to Ethiopia. During what would appear to have been a sojourn in Jerusalem, Frumentius apparently met, among others, Queen Helena, the devoted mother of the Emperor Constantine, who was then engaged in building the famous church of the capital, Holy Sepulcher, for which she was so widely renowned. Being deeply impressed by Frumentius's account of the great potentialities for the development of the Christian church in Ethiopia, Queen Helena is said to have urged Frumentius to go to Alexandria and make a detailed report of his experiences and observations to Archbishop Athanasius, who was then second only to the pope himself in power and influence in the Christian church.

Soon afterwards, Frumentius arrived in Alexandria and found Athanasius presiding over a synod, where the affairs of the church were being discussed with great earnestness. The young traveler was kindly received by Athanasius, who invited him to appear before the Council of Bishops and tell his story. After describing his experiences in Ethiopia and reviewing the possibilities for the establishment and growth of the Christian church there, Frumentius recommended that a bishop with a suitable staff be sent as soon as possible to Axum to promote the advancement of the Christian cause. Athanasius and his fellow bishops considered Frumentius's observations and recommendations with considerable care and concluded that they should be accepted and implemented without delay. Athanasius then sent for Frumentius and advised him of that decision. And in casting about for a suitable person for the new post, Athanasius and the bishops decided that no one was more qualified for that role than was Frumentius, who was ordained as a priest and consecrated as an archbishop; he then was appointed the primate of the envisioned Christian church in Ethiopia. Unfortunately, the exact date of this event is unknown, but according to church historian Socrates, Frumentius was appointed archbishop of Ethiopia a few years after Athanasius was consecrated as patriarch of Alexandria, which occurred around 326. On the strength of this fact, it is usually thought that Frumentius's consecration occurred at some time during the next decade (326–336) following Athanasius's elevation to the See of Alexandria.

Like the date of his consecration as archbishop of Ethiopia, the specific year in which Frumentius returned to Axum is rather uncertain; but it must have been several months, or perhaps longer, before 341. But whenever it was, his return to the country would seem to have been a veritable personal triumph. The members of the Christian community, in whose behalf he had labored so earnestly before leaving the country, took the lead in welcoming him on his return. But the warmth of his reception on that occasion was by no means limited to those who were already adherents of the Christian faith. The available testimony indicates that he was well received not only by the public at large but by the noble and princely classes, including his two former companions and students, the brothers Ezana and Shaiazana, who were then the co-rulers of the land. Whatever may have been their secret inclinations, it is certain that neither Ezana nor Shaiazana was a publicly professed Christian at the time of Frumentius's return. This is evidenced by statements in certain commemorative stelae in which both brothers proclaimed themselves to be devotees of gods who had been worshipped in the country long before the beginning of the Christian Era. In one inscription dating from the earlier part of his reign, Ezana called himself son of the war god (Mahram), and he invoked other pagan divinities— Astar, the moon god, and Medr, the earth god—to give him strength and to bless his reign. However, in another inscription, apparently dating from the latter part of his reign, there is no reference to the early gods; indeed, Ezana proclaimed himself a devotee of the "Lord of Heaven":

> Through the might of the Lord of Heaven, who is victorious in Heaven and on earth over all! Aezanes, the son of Ella Amida, of the tribe Halen, the king of Axum and Himyar and of Raidan and of Saba and of Salhen and of Siyamo and of Bega and of Kasu, the King of Kings, the son of Ella Amida, who will not be defeated by the enemy. Through the might of the Lord of Heaven, who has created me, of the Lord of All by whom the king is beloved, who will not be defeated by the enemy . . .

In several other places in the same inscription Ezana refers to the "power of the Lord of Heaven" as the force behind his successes. Ezana's coins reveal a similar transition in religious beliefs. Some coins, believed to date from his early years of rule, were stamped with circles and crescents which were symbols of cults promoting the worship of the sun and moon. But on later coins the Greek or Maltese cross replaced the sun and moon symbols.

Although both Ezana and Shaiazana did, in due course, publicly accept the Christian religion, it is generally assumed by modern scholars that the commemorative stelae were set up in the city of Axum before the two brothers took that momentous step. Notwithstanding the fact that neither of the two kings was an ostensible Christian when Frumentius began his labors as the official apostle to the Ethiopians, it is reasonably certain that both of the brothers were unsparing in their support of his efforts from the very start. It is not surprising, therefore, that the evangelical endeavors of Ethiopia's first archbishop were, as traditions relate, an overwhelming success.

Whether Frumentius's chief base of operation was located in the city of Axum itself or elsewhere in that general vicinity is a matter of some uncertainty. But it may be pointed out in this connection that, at a distance of about twelve miles east of Axum, there once existed a famous religious center named Fremona, from which the Portuguese directed much of their proselytizing activities in the fifteenth and sixteenth centuries when they were endeavoring to transform Ethiopia from a Coptic to a Roman Catholic state. And as the learned Jesuit historian Balthazar Telles has noted, the name Frumentius was spelled and pronounced in the Ethiopian language as Fremonatos. On the strength of this, Telles suggested that the word Fremona well may have been derived from the Ethiopian rendition of the name of their first archbishop. Carrying the matter a step further, Telles thought it not unlikely that the religious center at Fremona was originally established by the Ethiopian archbishop "Fremonatos," and that it was the main base from which his exceptionally successful evangelical program was carried out. For we are told that through the archbishop's labors in this "virgin vineyard of the Lord . . . great numbers were converted to the law of Christ." The situation has been aptly summarized: the Ethiopians "received the Doctrine of Holiness as the dry earth receives rain from heaven."

As a consequence of the widespread and astonishingly favorable response to Frumentius's ministrations, the newly established Ethiopian church was before many months numbering its adherents first by the thousands and then by the tens of thousands; and in this great army of converts were recruits representing all levels of Ethiopian society. Before many years had passed, the rank and file of the recently established church had come to include not only a countless host of underprivileged peasants, commoners, and budding plutocrats drawn from the masses, but most of the privileged princes and both of the reigning royal brothers as well. Although, as noted earlier, neither Ezana nor Shaiazana was a professing Christian at the time when Frumentius reappeared in Axum, both were subsequently converted and publicly baptized by the archbishop, and most of the nobility hastened to follow the royal lead. Thus, by 341 A.D. or thereabouts, which was hardly less than a decade after Frumentius had returned to Ethiopia, Christianity was so firmly established in the country that Ezana with scarcely a ripple of opposition established the new religion as the official faith of the ancient empire. So receptive were both the Ethiopian masses and classes to their great apostle for the spiritual service which he had rendered them, that he was elevated to sainthood and became an honored legend in his own lifetime, and has so remained in the national memory until this very day.

It should be stressed, however, that there was already a considerable Christian population in Axum at that time, so that the labors of Frumentius, backed by the kings and the court, made official and accelerated the conversion of large numbers of new believers. There is now available no historical document which specifically states that it was Frumentius who converted Ezana and his court, and who induced the king to make the faith the official religion of the kingdom, but all the available evidence suggests strongly that this was the case. It would appear that these developments occurred sometime between 330 and 340 A.D. An Ethiopian source suggests, but does not state, that these events took place about the year 333 A.D.

There is in the Ethiopian annals no name that has been longer and more widely revered than that of "Saint Fremonatos," who has also been endearingly immortalized by the Ethiopians as Abba Salama, which is variously translated as the "Father of Salvation," the "Father of Peace," or the "Father of Life." It should also be noted that the honors paid to Saint Frumentius have been confined by no means to the Church and nation in whose behalf he spent the greater part of his life. This is indicated by the fact that in former times most of the Christians of the world commemorated his memory by a special feast day bearing his name. In Ethiopia itself and perhaps also in Nubia, Egypt, and part of the Middle East, where the Coptic church flourished, this occurred on September twenty-third. In the Greek church,

Saint Frumentius's Day was commemorated on November thirtieth; while in the Roman church it fell on October twenty-seventh. Most historians who have given special attention to these recorded events have been deeply impressed with the unusually peaceful manner in which Saint Frumentius and King Ezana succeeded in making Christianity the national religion of what is Christendom's second oldest independent state. Writing in this connection, Sir Francis B. Head, the noted biographer of James Bruce (the earliest and one of the great modern European travelers in Ethiopia) has specifically observed that "never did the seed of the Christian religion find more genial soil than when it first fell among the rugged mountains of Abyssinia." There was, he states, "no war to introduce it, no fanatic priesthood to oppose it, no bloodshed to disgrace it; its only argument was its truth; its only ornament was its simplicity; and around our religion, thus shining in its native lustre, men flocked in peaceful humility, and hand in hand, joined cheerfully in doctrines which gave glory to God in the Highest, and announced on earth peace, goodwill toward men."

With the same basic thought in mind, Louis J. Morie, the learned, if nowadays little remembered, author of *Histoire de l'Ethiopie* many years ago characterized King Ezana as the "Clovis of Ethiopia," but he hastened to add that although the Ethiopian king was less well known in the western world than the royal patron of Christianity in medieval France, he was nonetheless a decidedly more humane and genial prince than was his notorious French counterpart. So far as Ezana's place in the early history of the Christian church is concerned, other writers have been wont to place Ethiopia's first Christian king in the same exclusive category as Constantine the Great.

The accolades which have been bestowed upon Saint Frumentius and his royal patron, King Ezana, do not mean that they had no detractors during the age in which they lived. Abba Salama in particular was denounced by some of his highly placed European contemporaries as one of the most wicked of men. This reflected the doctrinal squabble which so sorely distracted the Christian church soon after Constantine made it the official guardian of the spiritual life of the Roman Empire. Despite the efforts made by the great Roman emperor at the Council of Nicaea (in 325) to formulate a creed to which all Christians could subscribe, his laudable labors were soon afterwards brought to naught by the bitter doctrinal disputes between Archbishop Arius and his partisans on the one hand and the great Patriarch Athanasius and his followers on the other. The struggle came to a climax when Constantius II, one of the sons and successors of Constantine, fell under the spell of Arius and at his behest endeavored to have Athanasius and all high churchmen who shared his point of view driven from office as criminals and heretics, and replaced by partisans of the Arian creed. In keeping with this grand plan, Athanasius was driven by imperial order from his See in Alexandria and superseded by an Arian priest named George.

Attention was next directed toward Ethiopia, which was then the largest and wealthiest of all Christian countries lying beyond the boundaries of the Roman Empire. Inasmuch as Frumentius, its archbishop, was the chief protégé of Athanasius, the Arians were particularly anxious to have him replaced by a churchman of their own persuasion. And as soon as possible, a determined attempt was made to transform their hopes into reality. The plan was enlarged to include also the budding Christian communities of southwestern Arabia, which by virtue of their nearness to Ethiopia were found to be influenced by the course of affairs in that country.

With these goals in mind, in about 356 A.D. a large embassy headed by a learned Arian named Theophilus, who had been born on an island near Ethiopia but educated in Constantinople, was sent by Emperor Constantius to Axum and the Kingdom of Himyar in southwestern Arabia for the purpose of trying to persuade the royal authorities in these countries to ally themselves with the Arian cause. In addition to a long letter from Constantius to Ezana and his co-ruling brother, the embassy is said also to have carried along for the royal personages many rich and valuable presents, including among other things two hundred horses of pure breed from the land of Cappadocia. When Ambassador Theophilus and his associates arrived at Axum where they were kindly received at the Ethiopian court, they delivered the presents and the letter from Constantius to Ezana and Shaiazana and discussed, no doubt, the purpose of their mission. Unfortunately, there have survived no documents specifically recording the royal brothers' reaction to the purpose of the imperial mission as it was expressed in Emperor Constantius's letter; but from what may be inferred from related documents which have survived, it is safe to assume that the two Ethiopian kings were truly astonished at the impertinence of the Roman potentate.

From a copy of the letter, the text of which has survived, we learn that Constantius, forgetting apparently that he was addressing himself to the head of an independent and sovereign state, requested in effect that "the charlatan Frumentius" not only be deposed as primate of the Ethiopian church, but sent with all possible haste to Egypt to be tried and judged by "the most venerable George," Patriarch of Alexandria, and other Egyptian bishops in whom had been placed the supreme authority for ordaining prelates and deciding other important affairs of the Christian church. The letter continued:

> For unless you will pretend to be ignorant of what all the world well knows, you must be aware of the fact that Frumentius was consecrated Archbishop of Ethiopia by Athanasius, who has been deposed from his office because of his crime and wickedness and who is now a vagabond roving from place to place, as if he hoped to lose his guilt by shifting his dwelling place from one country to another.

It has been suggested by some modern scholars that Constantius's disparaging remarks about Athanasius are to be explained in part by his fear that the deposed Egyptian patriarch had fled, or was planning to flee, to seek the assistance of the Ethiopians in an effort to regain his position as primate of the church; by labeling both Frumentius and Athanasius as criminals, the Roman emperor hoped to discourage the Ethiopians from taking up the cudgels in their defense. Be that as it may, of one thing we are sure, and that is the fact that the Axumite potentates made no effort whatever to comply with the Roman emperor's request. Athanasius was not in Axum, as Constantius was inclined to suspect, but was then hiding in an Egyptian oasis in the desert west of the Nile. King Ezana, it seems, was aware of this fact, for it is known that he sent a copy of the Roman emperor's letter to the former patriarch, who subsequently incorporated it in his famous *Apology to Constantius*, which has survived intact and is the means by which the letter has come down to us. Frumentius was not sent to Egypt, as Constantius had requested, but remained in Ethiopia where he continued to enjoy the full confidence and support of his royal hosts and the Ethiopian people at large.

As had been the practice ever since Christianity had been made the state religion, crown lands were set aside and donations were made from the royal treasury to be used by the Abba Salama in whatever way he and his associates deemed fit. Some of the revenues deriving from such sources were utilized in building churches and residential establishments for the priesthood in various parts of the kingdom. Names of and traditions about some of the churches that are said to have been built during this period have been preserved in the national annals, and parts of a few of the buildings themselves are to be seen at the present day. The Church of Abba Hasabo is usually included in such a list. The two most famous of the churches which are said to date back to this period are the original Saint Mary of Sion

at Axum and what was formerly the Church of the Virgin
Mary, Queen of the Angels, on an ancient site in the modern
city of Massawa. The existing Church of Saint Mary of Axum
is a comparatively recent structure which is said to have been
built in the sixteenth century and is therefore only about
four hundred years old. On the same foundations, however,
there formerly stood an older church which bore the same
name. This structure, so tradition avows, was built under the
direction of Frumentius and the sponsorship of Ezana and
his royal brother and is said to have been erected around
340–341. Tradition further holds that this particular church
was itself preceded by a still older building or temple dedicated to the worship of the sun, and that it had been erected
by Queen Makeda, the queen of Sheba. Whether or not
these traditions are true is a matter which cannot be definitely determined. There is, however, a considerable amount
of traditional testimony—some of it perhaps epochal—as well
as a certain amount of archaeological evidence that would
seem to indicate that the church which was allegedly built
by Frumentius and Ezana was a historical fact. A description of this church is recorded in the *Book of Axum*. And
according to an ancient tradition, it was modeled after the
original Church of the Holy Sepulcher, which was built in
Jerusalem by Saint Helena, the mother of Constantine, between the years 330 and 336.

This ancient church would seem still to have been
standing twelve hundred years later when the famous mission, sent out by the king of Portugal, visited the country
between 1521 and 1526. Francisco Alvarez, who was the
chaplain and secretary of this mission, recorded in his remarkable history of the mission some interesting eyewitness
observations on a great church which stood on the same site
at that time and which was apparently the same edifice
which Frumentius and Ezana are said to have built. It was,
says Alvarez, "a very large and very noble church . . . it had
five naves of good width and great length." Each nave is

described as having a vaulted ceiling which was covered with paintings. The walls of the naves were also covered with paintings, and the floors were well worked with handsome cut stones. The church is said to have stood in a large walled enclosure, a part of which was "paved with flagstones like gravestones." Within this enclosure, so Alvarez stated, were "handsome terraced buildings" on all of which were "large figures of lions and dogs fashioned out of stone," out of the mouths of which water spouted during the rainy season. These buildings contained, no doubt, residential quarters for priests and monks and others who served the church in one capacity or another. Whether these buildings were as old as the church itself is a question, but in all likelihood they were not. A few years after Alvarez's visit, this whole complex of buildings, including the great church itself, was destroyed by Moslem invaders equipped with firearms, who thus were able to reduce much of the country to ruin before they were finally halted and crushed. After the war was over, a new but apparently smaller church was built on the foundations of the older one, and this structure with occasional restorations in later times has remained in existence until the present day.

If the Church of the Virgin Mary, Queen of the Angels, in Massawa in Eritrea, was indeed originally built, as tradition avows, in Saint Frumentius's time, it was one of the oldest churches in the ancient land. That this may have been in truth the case is indicated by the fact that this church has enjoyed a degree of sanctity that is matched by few other churches in the country. Tradition states that when it was built, Archbishop Frumentius designated it as a place of asylum, and that despite the many vicissitudes through which it and many of the surrounding churches in the country have passed, the church never lost its character in this respect.

When Eritrea was transformed into a Moslem country toward the end of the Middle Ages, the church was changed into a mosque and its name was changed to the Mosque of Sheik-el-Hammal. Its privileged position as a place of asylum is said, however, not to have been affected by these changes, for it is recorded that even after it was transformed into a mosque, anyone (a Moslem, a Christian, or a pagan) who took refuge in its precincts and lighted a candle there, was safe from harm. The lighting of a candle as a requisite to the privilege of asylum would seem to suggest that the practice dated back to some ancient Christian rite, and may have been instituted by Abba Salama himself. There are, moreover, reasons for believing that the granting of asylum under the circumstances just described was a kind of practice which the royal brothers and particularly Ezana would have fully approved. For there is, relatively speaking, a considerable amount of documentary evidence that clearly indicates that Ezana was a man of deep humanitarian impulses and great nobleness of heart, even before he became a Christian. Moreover, there is every reason to suppose that these benign elements in his character were broadened and intensified after he had publicly committed himself to ordering his life in accordance with the teachings of Christ.

For most of the documented details concerning Ezana's career, both before and after he became a Christian, we are indebted to a series of remarkable historical inscriptions which are engraved on large stelae, or tablets of stone, and which had been originally set up by the great king in the capital city of Axum for the purpose of commemorating a number of the notable events of his reign. Three of these inscriptions are written in an ancient and indigenous script and language known to the Ethiopians as Ge'ez, but frequently called Ethiopic. Another of the inscriptions is written in Sabaean, one of the ancient languages of southwestern Arabia, which maintained rather close relationships with Ethiopia for many centuries. Still another of the inscriptions is written in Greek, a fact which should not be surprising when it is remembered that Greeks or Greek-speaking people are known to have maintained close contacts with the country for several hundred years. Indeed, a number of the kings from the first through the sixth centuries are known to have been well versed in Greek. There were other Ethiopians, no doubt, including traders and government officials, who possessed varying degrees of facility in the language. The trilingual character of these inscriptions, and there must have been others which have not survived, recalls the fact that in one of them Ezana indicates that he had caused them to be set up in order that men of many nations might know of his deeds and the glory of his kingdom forever. And it may be said, in this connection, that history bears witness that his hopes in these respects are being abundantly fulfilled.

Although most of these inscriptions and the events which they record were almost wholly forgotten by all except some Ethiopians, this unhappy situation has undergone a radical change during the nineteenth and twentieth centuries. The change began in 1808 when Henry Salt, a learned and enterprising English traveler and antiquarian, visited the ancient and ruined city of Axum and found three of these inscriptions, which he published in part, first in 1811 and again in 1814. Another of the inscriptions was first seen and copied in Axum by the German traveler and naturalist Wilhelm Ruppell in 1833. Then came yet another discovery, also in the city of Axum, by that noted English wayfarer, James Theodore Bent, in 1893. Finally there occurred the remarkable discoveries and studies by the great German-Aksum Archaeological Expedition under the direction of Enno Littmann, in the city of Axum in 1906.

In addition to the attention given to them by antiquarians and archaeologists who first brought them to light, all of these inscriptions have subsequently been studied, restudied, and translated by numerous scholars versed in the languages in which they were written. The texts have been published in translated form in most of the major literary languages of the Western world, and as a consequence of these activities, the now available primary sources of information on King Ezana are surpassed in quantity by comparable materials relating to few, if any of the other great personalities of his age.

III

Ethiopia's Early Development as a Christian State

The success of the Ethiopian church resulted essentially from three factors: the diligent work of early missionaries, a flexibility in the early policy of church leaders, and the support of Ethiopian kings. There was probably a constant flow of Christian immigrants into Ethiopia following the emergence of the faith, but the condemnation of Monophysites by the Council of Chalcedon and the general persecutions in the Byzantine Empire during the fifth century greatly accelerated the stream of Christian refugees into the country. Many of those immigrants not only taught and preached Christianity, they also established Christian communities in several parts of the country, and some of them even participated in affairs of state. The missionary tactics of these early proselytizers included the use of traditional temples for worship and the acceptance of certain customary practices of the people, both of which minimized the impact of the religious changes taking place. And since continued missionary and educational growth required economic support, the early Christians were fortunate to have received several large royal grants of tax-exempt lands which the king could not *reappropriate; in this way, the church became a wealthy landowner. This in itself had tremendous consequences for the evolution of Ethiopian society; but of equal significance is the fact that the church became both an ally which reinforced the monarchy, and a unifying force among Ethiopians. Indeed, the church emerged as the principal institution upon which most Ethiopians relied for their spiritual, economic, and cultural sustenance.*

The key aspects of these strategic developments in Ethiopia's history are described by Professor Hansberry in the following essay.

The Editor

Anyone familiar with the course of affairs in the Roman Empire under the early Christian emperors will readily acknowledge that the decrees of Constantine had scarcely freed Christians from persecution by their pagan enemies before they began to persecute one another with the most unrelenting fury. The strife between Christian and Christian, which began while Constantine was still alive, continued with increasing intensity for the next three hundred years and was one of the primary causes, if not the primary cause, of the debilitated condition in which the Roman Empire found itself during the closing centuries of historical antiquity.

At the same time that the Roman Empire was undergoing these traumatic experiences which did so much to undermine its strength and internal cohesiveness at home and to dissipate the power and influence which it had so long exercised in world affairs, the newly established Christian kingdom of Ethiopia was passing through an era of great peace and prosperity at home, and unparalleled influence and prestige abroad. As paradoxical as it may at first appear, Christian Ethiopia's internal and external development during this period was, in no small degree, a reflex of the internal weaknesses and demoralizing conditions then prevailing in most of the rest of the Christian world. This view is confirmed by the following examination of some of the specific historical events and developments during the formative period of Ethiopia's Christian existence.

When Ezana and Shaiazana died in 356 or thereabouts, they were succeeded by three of the latter's sons, who are best known to history as Ela Abreha II, Ela Asfeha, and Ela Shahel II. These three brothers are said to have been jointly and simultaneously elevated to the throne with equal authority in imperial affairs. If tradition is to be believed, the division of authority among them was achieved by dividing the day into three equal parts, with each brother governing unhampered by the other two during the time allotted to him.

As a consequence of this arrangement, the joint reign is said to have been without friction, and the three brothers are reputed to have lived in close harmony throughout the period of their occupancy of the throne. While we cannot be sure of the extent to which this delicate and possibly dangerous division of the imperial authority was due to the influence of Abba Salama, it seems reasonable to assume that the Christian spirit, of which he was such an able exponent, played no inconsiderable part in determining the decidedly peaceful character of this potentially discordant fraternal relationship. Christian friction at the international level, however, increasingly involved Ethiopia.

Soon after Constantine's death, Arius, a native of Libya and a priest of Alexandria whose version of Christian doctrines had been condemned at the Council of Nicaea in 325 A.D., won the favor of Constantius, the more fanatical of Constantine's successors. With the young Emperor's backing, Arius inaugurated a campaign of persecution against his fellow Christians who had previously rejected the tenets which he had espoused as the proper creed of the infant church. This campaign embraced the whole of the Roman Empire, but it was expressed with exceptional severity in Egypt, Libya, and other North African countries then under Roman rule. But as noted previously, the celebrated Archbishop of the Egyptian church, Athanasius, who was Arius's chief opponent, was with imperial approval deposed and banished, and many of the bishops under his administration were either murdered or forced to flee for safety to Nubia, Ethiopia, and other parts of Africa beyond the reach of the Roman authorities. Many of the ordinary communicants of the churches over which Athanasius and his bishops had presided were also victims of Arian attack. In Alexandria, as elsewhere in Egypt, their churches were closed, destroyed, or appropriated by Arius and his supporters. Among the laity who were seized and imprisoned before they could flee, some renounced their allegiance to the orthodox church and allied themselves with the Arian sect; but those who refused to save themselves by such measures were condemned to the mines and stone quarries. Those who succeeded in fleeing the country and thereby escaping the torment of their fellow Christians of the Arian persuasion often forfeited all rights in the personal properties which they left behind; and, not infrequently, those of their kindred on whom the Arians could lay hands were victimized in various ways.

The chief instigator of these atrocities against his fellow Christians (as well as against pagans) was "the most venerable George" to whom the Emperor Constantius referred in his letter dispatched to Ezana and Shaiazana in 356 A.D. (see p. 76). It will be recalled that Constantius requested in this letter that the two royal Ethiopian brothers send Archbishop Frumentius to Egypt to be tried for heresy by the venerable George and his Arian associates. It will be further recalled that the Ethiopian kings refused to grant this request. Although the Roman Emperor was mistaken in thinking that Athanasius had fled or was planning to flee to Ethiopia, there are good reasons for believing that many of the outlawed partisans of the deposed patriarch were granted religious asylum in the country at that time.

With Christian influences entering Ethiopia under such varied and inauspicious circumstances, it is remarkable that the new religion should have taken such deep and firm roots in the country in such a relatively short period. For in less than two hundred years after the establishment of Christianity as the state religion, Ethiopia, by the beginning of the sixth century, had attained a level of internal development and acquired a degree of external influence which placed it on a par with the Byzantine Empire as one of the greatest Christian powers of that age.

We are indebted to Saint Jerome (circa 340–420), who was one of the earliest and most learned of the Latin Fathers of the Church, for an apparently reliable testimony concerning the rapid growth of Christianity in Ethiopia during the early part of the period. The reference here is to two statements which have come down to us by way of published copies of letters written by Saint Jerome to friends in Rome. During the time when he was in Palestine and engaged in preparing the famous Latin, or Vulgate, translation of the Bible, he mentions in one of these letters addressed to his friend Marcellus that Ethiopia was a country "abounding in monks." In another letter dispatched to a noble Roman lady and friend, he recommended that she send her daughter to Palestine to be instructed by monks from India, Persia, and Ethiopia, because "we daily receive" from these countries, "troops of monks" who are known as "lilies of purity."

The noted Jesuit historian Balthazar Telles quoted with approval an observation by a fellow countryman, Don Alfonso Mendez, that the Ethiopian monks mentioned by Saint Jerome were in all likelihood inmates or products of monastic establishments which had been set up in Ethiopia by Frumentius, who had been accompanied to the country by some "tried monks of exemplary lives bred up under Saint Anthony," one of the founders of monasticism. Following their arrival they established monasteries and many monks went to Palestine to visit the holy places.

If Telles was correct in suggesting that the great Jesuit religious center at Fremona owed its origin to Frumentius, this could well have been one of the monastic establishments from which fared forth the monks to whom Saint Jerome referred. Exactly when Saint Jerome penned this epistle is not indicated; but since he is known to have lived in Palestine from about 385 A.D. to his death in 420, the letters were no doubt written some time between these two dates. If, therefore, Saint Jerome's remarks may be taken at their face value, Ethiopia must have been abounding in monks within less than a century after Christianity was recognized as the official religion of the country.

Although Ethiopian Christians would appear to have

avoided at home the doctrinal disputes and attendant religious strife which proved so disruptive to the early Christian church, they or their representatives were not always able to escape involvement in such struggles elsewhere, in other parts of the Christian world. A striking instance in this connection occurred early in the fifth century when John Chrysostom, the Patriarch of Constantinople and widely regarded by his contemporaries and in later times as "the most illustrious orator and doctor of the early Church," championed certain teachings by the great Origen which had been declared anathema by some of the leading orthodox churchmen of the age. Theophilus, the Patriarch of Alexandria, was particularly incensed by what he regarded as Chrysostom's unorthodox views and resolved to have his brother patriarch removed from high office. About the same time the illustrious orator and archbishop made another mistake by referring to the luxury-loving Empress Eudoxia as a Byzantine Jezebel. Using these two mistakes, particularly the latter, Theophilus, accompanied by Egyptian and Ethiopian bishops, hastened to Constantinople and, with the assistance of the injured empress, succeeded in 403 A.D. in convening a conference known in history as the Synod of the Oaks. Chrysostom was tried by this synod, found guilty, deposed, and then banished to a gloomy and isolated outpost in the Caucasus Mountains.

Among the more notable events which relate to Ethiopia's early relations with Western Christendom is a statement in the *Chronicle of John of Nikiu* to the effect that the Ethiopian king sent a message to "the God-loving Emperor Honorius" (395–423) requesting that he send Ethiopians a bishop to administer to their spiritual needs. The emperor "rejoiced with great joy" on learning that these Ethiopians had "embraced the Faith and turned to God." In response to their request he sent them a bishop named Theonius who admonished and instructed them and strengthened their faith in Christ. If the king mentioned here was the "king of

kings" in Axum rather than a sub-king living in Ethiopia, and
if the statement is otherwise approximately true, it is of more
than usual historical significance. For up to that time all of
Ethiopia's relationships with Roman Christians had been
with those living in the eastern provinces of the Roman Empire. But this is an instance in which a request for religious
assistance was directed to the Roman west, where theological
doctrines were already taking on aspects significantly different from those in the East to which the Ethiopians had, in
the main, subscribed. Indeed, this incident would seem to
suggest that the Ethiopians were not particularly concerned
about the niceties of theological dogmas prevailing in the
countries from which outside religious assistance was se-
cured—all that seemed to matter was that they be well
grounded in the cardinal principles of the Christian faith.

How little the Ethiopians permitted themselves to be
troubled by doctrinal differences which were the cause of so
much tension and stress among Christians elsewhere is illus-
trated by the freedom of movement and hospitality accorded to Palladius of Galatia, a wandering heretic and
exile who visited Ethiopia about the same time that the
western Roman Emperor Honorius is alleged to have dispatched a religious mission to the country. Palladius (368–
431) was the bishop of a provincial city in Asia Minor and
a friend and partisan of John Chrysostom. Shortly afterwards and on charges similar to those against Chrysostom,
Palladius was also deposed from his post and banished. His
last place of confinement was in Aswan on the boundary
between Egypt and Nubia. After his release, he traveled for
some time in Nubia and then in Ethiopia where eventually
he appeared in the then important port city of Adulis.

Sometime after his arrival there, he met and became a
close friend of Moses, the Bishop of the Ethiopian church
in that city. During the period of their association, Palladius
and the Ethiopian bishop worked out arrangements for making a joint sea journey to India for the purpose of investi-

gating the religion and philosophy of the Brahmins. In due course, the two friends set sail in one of the vessels engaged in trade between Ethiopia and India. From there Palladius eventually made his way back to Egypt where it would appear that he remained until his death in 431. As interesting as this story is as a travelogue, its main importance lies in the fact that it reveals a broad view toward non-Christian philosophy on the part of Palladius and of Bishop Moses, a rare view at that time.

In the same year that Palladius died, there occurred at Ephesus in Asia Minor an event which was to have significant repercussions not only in Ethiopia but throughout much of western and central Asia as well. The Ephesian episode grew out of a theological dispute in which most of the leading churchmen of the time were eventually involved. In 428 an able though rather intolerant Syrian priest, Nestorius, was elected patriarch of Constantinople, and shortly after his elevation launched a crusade against all Christian sects with whose tenets he did not agree. About two years after his elevation, he took a step which caused him to fall into even greater disfavor. In the course of a sermon in the Great Church of Constantinople, Anastasius, a priest under Nestorius' administration, startled his audience by denying that the Virgin Mary could be truly called the mother of God, for Mary was, he contended, a human creature and God could not be the offspring of a human being.* The priest insisted that Jesus, the son of Mary, was not truly God but merely a man so superabundantly blessed and inspired that he could not sin. In essence, this view held that the divine and human

---

* Based on the Council of Nicaea (325) the Ethiopians accepted the position that Christ is fully God and man, that Christ is of the same nature as God (consubstantial), and that there was never a time when Christ did not exist (condemnation of a view taken by Arianism). At the Council of Ephesus (431) the Ethiopians agreed that Mary is the mother of God, since it was from her that God received humanity in the form of Christ.

natures of Christ are separate. Most high-ranking churchmen in Constantinople and elsewhere took violent exception
to this view, but the Patriarch Nestorius supported the cou-
rageous and independent-minded priest, and in 431 Nestorius was tried by the Council of Ephesus, convicted of
heresy, deposed, excommunicated, and then banished first
to Arabia and later to the Egyptian desert west of the Nile.
There he was placed under the surveillance of an unorthodox Christian community that was guarded by a Roman gar-
rison. He eventually succeeded in returning to some of his
Levantine followers who protected him from further persecution until his death in 451.

Nestorius' excommunication, banishment, and death did
not put an end to the influence of his teachings. On the
contrary, Christians who agreed with his objections to call-
ing the Virgin Mary the mother of God rapidly increased in
number and despite their persecution, they formed themselves into an organized church which eventually spread its
influence throughout western and southern Asia and eastward as far as China. Nestorian missionaries are known to
have introduced Christianity into parts of central Asia in the
tenth century, and some authorities have contended that it
was Nestorian missionaries rather than the apostles Thomas
and Bartholomew, as tradition avows, who actually established the "Christian community of St. Thomas" in Malabar
on the western coast of India.

One Nestorian achievement in Asia led to much con-
fusion in later times concerning Ethiopia's place in world
history during the Middle Ages. This was their conversion
of the Mongol Karith, whose king Ung Khan received the
title Malik Juchana (King John) following his baptism.
Later, when Latin crusaders in the Holy Land heard echoes
of the existence of a powerful and vastly wealthy Christian
king "in the East," some of them concluded that the powerful and wealthy Christian king of whom they were beginning to hear must be the Mongol Ung Khan (King John). In

due course, echoes of this mighty Christian king began to reverberate, and eventually he acquired the title, "Prester John." Acting on this hazy identification, various papal and princely missions were sent out to Asia with the hope of locating this phantom Prester John, who in fact reigned in Ethiopia.

The Council of Ephesus influenced the history of Ethiopia in still another manner. As has already been indicated, many Christians who adopted the Nestorian point of view were often the objects of scorn, ridicule, and even persecution by fellow Christians, and sought relief from their unhappy positions by flight into other lands. Many of these refugees fled to Ethiopia for asylum, and some of them contributed substantially to the growth of Christianity in their adopted land. In 451, the year in which Nestorius is believed to have died, there occurred another conference of churchmen, the Council of Chalcedon, the aftermath of which had a particularly significant influence upon the growth of Christianity in Ethiopia. This Council supported the view that Christ is of two natures, divine and human. The Egyptian rejection of this decree and the severance of all official relationships with both the Church of Constantinople and the Church of Rome led to the establishment of the Coptic Church of Egypt. The Ethiopian Christians who had been intimately associated with the Egyptian church ever since the days of the great Athanasius continued that historical relationship and maintained their philosophy of consubstantialism. The Egyptian Coptic Christians and the Ethiopian Christians became the leaders of a new group, the Monophysites.

As was the case following the actions taken by the Council of Ephesus, there were many Christians in Syria and elsewhere in the eastern provinces of the Roman Empire who refused to accept the decrees of the Council of Chalcedon, but in as much as these decrees represented the orthodox position of the church and had the official sanction of

the government, those who opposed those Chalcedon decisions found themselves being regarded as traitors and heretics by many of their Christian fellowmen. Thus, in order to
escape their precarious positions, many sought security in
new homes beyond the reach of the imperial law. The country that offered them greatest advantages in these respects
was Ethiopia, and in the course of the next decade or two
a considerable number of Christians from the eastern part
of the Roman Empire availed themselves of that African
country's hospitality.

Among these Christian refugees were some who made
such a profound impression on their Ethiopian contemporaries that the memory of the group became an integral part
of the national tradition and their story has been preserved
to the present day. Some chose as dwelling places natural
caves or rock shelters, and for food they depended almost
entirely upon herbs and wild fruits and were thankful for
whatever nature supplied in these respects. As a general rule
they cut themselves off from all human contact and forgot
their loneliness in prayer and religious thought. About one
hundred years after their arrival in the country, the Ethiopian King Gabra Maskal I, who reigned from about 545 to
about 580 A.D., dedicated a church at Baraknaha to their
memory. At this site there is to be seen at the present day
a small church tucked away in a cramped ravine, almost hidden from public view by the foliage of trees and screening
vines. It is unlikely that this church, though obviously quite
old, is the same structure that was built in Gabra Maskal's
time, but the site on which it stands is believed to be that of
the church built in memory of the devout ascetics. None of
those refugees is known to history, but oddly enough what
are believed to be the bodies of some of them have been preserved at Amba-Fokada near Matara in Eritrea. The partly
mummified bodies and bones of a number of human beings
are kept in a small chapel and are said by tradition to rep-
resent the mortal remains of those devoted holy men who

dwelt in these regions when Christianity in Ethiopia was young.

There were some refugees who took an exceptionally active part in promoting the growth of Christianity in their adopted homeland, and their names have been well-known to, and greatly revered by, all of Ethiopia's many Christians. The most renowned of these have long been known collectively as the "Nine Saints," and their names are usually recorded in historical tradition as follows: Abba Afse, Abba Alef, Abba Shema, Abba Guba, Abba Garima, Abba Yemata, Abba Aragawi (or Mikael or Michael), Abba Likanos, and Abba Pantalewon.

Exactly when these nine saints entered Ethiopia, where they came from, and whether they migrated in one group or as individual wayfarers are matters that have never been determined to the satisfaction of all scholars concerned. Most students of the question have been disposed to think that the immigrants were Syrian Monophysites who fled their country as individual refugees at different times during the first two or three decades of the last half of the fifth century, although it is generally agreed that one of them, Abba Pantalewon, was probably a Monophysite from Egypt. Most and perhaps all of them were apparently learned ecclesiastics with a penchant for the cloistered life, although they seem to have taken an active part in public affairs as well. It is widely acknowledged that as scholars they added greatly to the Christian literature then available in Ethiopia by translating the scriptures and other noted religious writings into Ge'ez (Ethiopic) which was then the principal literary language used in the church and at the court. It is believed that the earliest of the translations were the Four Gospels, followed by selected sections of the Old and New Testaments. Added to these were certain religious or quasi-religious works, such as Palladius' *Garden of the Fathers* and certain biographical writings treating the lives of the martyrs and saints of earlier times. A number of secular writings, most of them long since lost, are believed to have been translated into Ge'ez from Greek, Latin, Coptic, and other languages during this same period. It is of interest to note that the Ethiopian editions of two of the works whose translations date from this period are the only versions of those works known to be still in existence. One of these is the *Book of Enoch* which was brought to England from Ethiopia by James Bruce in 1773; and the other was a translation into Ethiopic of the so-called *Romance of Alexander the Great*, which was based on an Egyptian version alleged to be a translation from a Greek original written by Callisthenes of Olynthus in the fourth century B.C. Though rather widely known in the Christian world in the Middle Ages, all known manuscripts of the Alexander story subsequently disappeared and remained unknown in Christian lands until British soldiers during the Napier invasion of Ethiopia in 1868 seized a copy of the Ethiopian version, along with hundreds of other manuscripts, and transported it to Europe during the following year.

But as important as their literary efforts were, the Nine Saints exercised an even greater influence on the development of Christianity in Ethiopia through their activities as preachers, builders of churches, and founders of monastic establishments. Abba Afse is credited with having established a religious center in an old traditional temple at Yeha which is situated a few miles to the northeast of the present town of Adowa. Abba Garima is said to have founded the ancient monastery of Medera, which lies to the southwest of the ancient Yeha. The founding of the monastery of Beagsa is credited to Abba Alef; while Abba Yemata is said to have built the monastery of Garalta.

The founders of the two most famous and influential of Ethiopia's ancient monasteries were Abba Likanos and Abba Aragawi, the latter known to tradition as St. Michael. Abba Likanos, who is thought by some to have lived in the great monastic establishment of Saint Pachomius at Tabenna in upper Egypt before coming to Ethiopia, was the founder of the famous and influential monastery of Debra Quonatsil, better known to history as the monastery of Debra Likanos in honor of the great preacher and scholar by whom it was built. Abba Likanos, reportedly of Byzantine origin, had the reputation of being a very learned man and is credited as the first to translate the Book of Psalms into the Coptic language. A number of architectural features seem to link the Debra Likanos monastery with the types of buildings that were common in the country in late antiquity and in early Christian times.

Following Abba Likanos' "withdrawal from the world" (which means no doubt his retirement from the active direction of his monastery) the learned father is said by Ethiopian tradition to have retired to a neighboring village, which today bears the name Guna-Guna, where he limited his activities to study, prayerful meditations, and religious devotions in a small church at that site. There is today at Guna-Guna a small church situated precariously high up on the face of a steep cliff and is very difficult to reach, but church services would seem to have been scarcely affected by this factor. How much of the present church at Guna-Guna was in existence in Abba Likanos' times is unknown; elsewhere in the same general vicinity, however, there is, in a more accessible place, a round church to which the Abba's name has been given. This church is a relatively modern structure, but it is erected on the foundations of an older church which probably bore the same honored name.

Of all the surviving buildings in Ethiopia which are associated in one way or another with Abba Likanos' career, none reflects more emphatically his enduring renown in the country than does a great monolithic church which was erected in his honor at Lalibela in the mountains of Lasta some seven hundred years after his death. This church bears the great ecclesiastic's name and was hewn entirely out of a vast mass of solid rock under the patronage and at the command of King Lalibela, who is believed to have reigned from 1170 to 1220, and erected on the same site ten other rock-hewn churches which rank among the Seven Wonders of the World.

Abba Aragawi, who according to available evidence did more to promote the growth of Christianity in ancient Ethiopia than any of the other Nine Saints, was the founder of the famous monastery of Debra Damo, which surpassed all of the other monasteries as a center of religious training in early Christian times and achieved its pre-eminence as Ethiopia's chief center of monastic learning, even though its location was more inaccessible than was the monastery of Abba Likanos or any of the other several monastic establishments then flourishing in the country.

The monastery of Debra Damo is important for another reason. On its summit there stands today a complex of buildings which have been rather carefully studied on the spot by a number of archaeologists, architects, and historians in recent decades and it has been generally agreed that the principal architectural remains at Debra Damo may date back to the end of the fifth or the beginning of the sixth century. If the church dates back to the fifth or sixth centuries, it is as ancient as the church of Saint Vitale in Ravenna, Italy, and the great cathedral church of Saint Sophia in Constantinople, and is therefore one of the oldest Christian churches of importance in the world. And even if it dates back no further than the eleventh century, as some critics believe, it is as old as most of the Romanesque and older than all of the Gothic cathedrals for which Christian Europe has been so long renowned.

Whatever its date, the church at Debra Damo has architectural and artistic features that have much in common with the architectural and artistic practices which preceded and followed those in vogue when Debra Damo was built. The architectural features in Debra Damo find striking parallels in monumental remains dating from the pre-Christian and early Christian periods as well as in the famous rock-hewn or monolithic churches at Lalibela.

In the course of the so-called Judith rebellion in the

tenth century, attempts were made to reach and destroy Debra Damo, but the inmates of the monastery only had to pull up the ropes, the only means by which ascent was possible, to save themselves and their church from their foes. Tradition reports that in the first half of the sixteenth century, hostile Muslim forces made an attempt to seize this ancient Christian edifice but they too found it impregnable. This, then, is part of the legacy of Debra Damo, which, with Debra Likanos, was the wealthiest and most influential of Ethiopian monasteries in the Middle Ages.

Of Abba Pantalewon, the last of the Nine Saints to be discussed here, tradition has handed down a number of interesting particulars. Surviving traditions do not credit him with having been the founder of any important monastic establishment, but mention is made of a number of churches which are said to have been erected in his honor. The ruins of one of these is situated in the outskirts of ancient Axum, and if correctly identified, they would seem to have been rather well preserved when the city of Axum was visited by Alvarez during the first quarter of the sixteenth century. In reporting his observations, Alvarez described it as "a very elegant small church of much devotion." It was surrounded by a wall of wrought masonry and was situated at the top of a peak and was reached, according to Alvarez, by climbing a flight of three hundred steps winding up the sides of the peak from its base to the top. Surrounding the church were "the sepulchers of saints," which reminded Alvarez of similar tombs which he had seen in Portugal.

PROTECTOR OF THE FAITH ABROAD

When their coreligionists in neighboring countries were unjustly attacked or otherwise mistreated by their non-Christian overlords, Nubian and Ethiopian armies were promptly dispatched to the aid of their brothers in the faith and on more than one occasion put an end to their distress. One of the most noted of the early instances in which Ethiopian armies assumed such a role as "defender of the faith" occurred in the Kingdom of Himyar, located in the southern Arabian peninsula. That intervention stemmed from the alleged violation of treaties of peace and friendship concluded by Emperor Anastasius and Justin I with the Kingdom of Himyar. Those treaties provided for the protection of Roman merchants passing through Himyar in the course of trade with India, the source of silks and other products for Byzantium. Such a treaty allowed the Byzantines to boycott similar products sold by their enemies, the Persians. *

During the reign of Himyar King Dhu Nuwas some Alexandrian merchants were murdered by some Himyarites, and this paved the way for Caleb's invasion of the kingdom in 519. The trade route with India crossed the Arabian peninsula (Himyar), linking Egypt, Nubia, and Axum by way of the Red Sea. This was indeed a crucial artery of the international trade of Africa, Asia, and Europe, the latter being linked to Egypt. The murder of the Alexandrian merchants threatened the security along an important link of that trade route and violated treaty agreements. In addition, some writers believed that the persecution of Christians by the Himyarites provided another reason for the Ethiopian invasion. Thus, in 519, Caleb's troops crossed the Red Sea, defeated Dhu Nuwas' army, installed a tributary (vassal) king, and returned to Ethiopia.

When Caleb's Himyar appointee died around 523, Dhu Nuwas came out of hiding, raised an army estimated at 70–120,000 men, and sought to re-establish his power. Some critics think Dhu Nuwas was leading a nationalist revolt

* As a Christian state, Ethiopia's role in international affairs was partly influenced by elements of the Queen of Sheba legend: first, King Solomon allegedly had a prophetic dream in which God's favor passed from Israel to Ethiopia; and second, the Ark of the Covenant was abducted and placed in Axum. Both of these allegations led Ethiopians to regard their country as the second Zion, with the monarch regarded as successor to Justin I of Byzantium (with whom Caleb of Ethiopia was an ally in the sixth century) as defender of the Christian faith.

against Ethiopian rule and that the Persians encouraged the movement as part of an anti-Byzantine program; there seems to be some justification for this view. But whatever the case, the conflict pitched anti-Christians against Christians, and Caleb was committed to protect the latter (but one should not underestimate the economic motives). Caleb had the support of Justin I, who sent a mission to urge the Ethiopian king to give aid to the Himyarite Christians.

Just before departing for the Arabian campaign, it is alleged, Caleb led a procession to a church in Axum and prayed for his people, himself, and the success of his mission. He also received the blessing of Saint Pantalewon. Thus blessed and reassured of his cause, Caleb and his nephew, Aryat, led an estimated force of 120,000 toward the Arabian coast in 525. The Ethiopian force was divided into two parts. One division landed on the Red Sea coast, or the western coast of Arabia, while the other part of the army was dispatched through the strait of Bab el Mandeb with the intention of landing on the southern coast of Arabia. It was Caleb's plan that these two armies, one approaching from the west towards the southeast and the other approaching from the south towards the northwest, would trap Dhu Nuwas' forces in a kind of pincer movement, forcing them to fight on two fronts at the same time. Unfortunately for the Ethiopians, this tactic miscarried. The part of the army which landed on the west coast experienced great hardship in endeavoring to traverse the desert areas which they had to cross to carry out the plan. While marching through the desert they were attacked by Dhu Nuwas' forces and were either destroyed or scattered.

The part of the Ethiopian army which Caleb had ordered to land on the southern coast of Arabia met with more success, but not without having experienced great risks and a determined attempt on Dhu Nuwas' part to prevent the consummation of the plan. In order to carry out their strategy it was necessary for the Ethiopian fleet

on the southern coast to pass through the strait of Bab el
Mandeb, which separates the eastern coast of Africa from
the southwestern tip of Arabia and which connects the
southernmost part of the Red Sea with the Gulf of Aden.
This narrow body of water is hazardous because of many
small and hidden islands and is perilous to navigation even
at the present day. (The dangers involved in navigating this
narrow and dangerous waterway are reflected in its present
name Bab el Mandeb, which means the "Gate of Tears," and
was so designated by ancient mariners because of the in-
numerable disasters which occurred there.)

It was through these treacherous waters that Caleb's
transports had to pass before the southern shores of Arabia
could be reached. Although Dhu Nuwas was well aware of
the great risk which the Ethiopians would run in endeavoring to send an expeditionary force by sea to southern Arabia,
he did not rely solely on natural dangers to safeguard his
kingdom from the Ethiopian invasion. On the contrary, he
made a bold and ingenious attempt to block the passage of
the Ethiopian ships through the narrow and dangerous strait.
(Although the strait is about three miles wide today, there
is a goodly bit of geographical evidence and traditional testimony to the effect that it was substantially less in width
when Dhu Nuwas conceived and tried to implement his
plan). Taking advantage of the narrowness of the strait, the
Himyarite king, so tradition avows, stretched a long, large,
and heavy chain of iron across the strait at its least dangerous part. The ends of the chain were firmly fixed and held
fast by heavy rocks on the opposite sides of the strait. The
chain was hidden from view by being stretched just below
the surface of the water, but high enough to entangle the
bottoms of the ships when they endeavored to pass. Having
completed this daring piece of strategy, Dhu Nuwas en-
camped with his army on the coast near where he expected
that the Ethiopians would attempt to disembark when they
discovered that the great chain was blocking their passage.

Before long Dhu Nuwas' scouts announced that the
Ethiopian armada was on its way. Soon thereafter it came
into sight and progressed to the point where the great chain
was stretched. Being unaware of the presence of the hidden
chain, the vanguard of the Ethiopian fleet, consisting of ten
ships, plowed forward quite innocently, and miraculously
passed over the obstruction without incident. Exactly what
had gone awry is not altogether clear, but it would appear
that at the moment the ships arrived the high tide was at its
peak, thus allowing the vanguard of the fleet to float over
Dhu Nuwas' obstruction. Some of the rear guard were halted
by the chain, however, no doubt the result of the tide having
ebbed by the time these ships arrived. A little later, however, the halted ships also passed successfully over the chain
and in due course joined the rest of the fleet which was
coasting along the south Arabian shore. The first ten ships
passed through Bab el Mandeb and landed near the present
port of Aden, with the intention of marching troops inland.
The remainder of the fleet, which had the greater part of the
expeditionary force aboard, sailed by Aden and landed a
considerable distance further to the east.

Dhu Nuwas, observing these developments, left behind
a small force to oppose the Ethiopians who had landed at
Aden while he himself, with the greater part of his army,
headed eastward to intercept the major body of the expeditionary force wherever it decided to land. The Ethiopian
divisions which had disembarked near Aden were under the
command of the nephew of the Ethiopian king, while the
larger force was commanded by Caleb himself.

In order to raise the fighting spirit of his soldiers to
maximum pitch, Aryat, so Arab sources inform us, caused
the ten ships from which they and their supplies had been
disembarked to be set on fire, and then addressed his troops
as follows: "Oh men of Ethiopia, before you are your enemies and behind you is the sea and there are no ships in
which you could take flight. Your choice, therefore, is vic-

tory over your foes or death at your enemies' hands!" Aryat
then commanded his army to advance. The small force
which had been left behind by Dhu Nuwas put up a stub-
born fight, but was at length wiped out or put to flight.
Aryat and his troops then hastened toward the metropolis
Zafar, which was wholly unprepared to resist an open attack
or to withstand the siege by closing its gates. The people of
Zafar therefore surrendered their city to the Ethiopians
without a fight.

While these developments were taking place, the main
expeditionary force under Caleb's command had landed well
to the east of Aden and was pushing forward into the in-
terior. Dhu Nuwas, while endeavoring to stop Caleb's advance, received word that Zafar had fallen into the enemy's
hands. He was, reports ancient tradition, truly astonished by
the swiftness and the effectiveness of the Ethiopians' military
operations, and the courage of his soldiers was reduced almost to the vanishing point. With Aryat marching against
him from one direction and Caleb and his forces approaching from the other, Dhu Nuwas now realized that he was
being threatened from all sides; but he resolved to make at
least one more desperate effort to save himself. In the skir-
mish which followed, he and his soldiers experienced a de-
cisive and disastrous defeat.

Traditions differ concerning Dhu Nuwas' fate after his
defeat. According to one account, it appears that he and his
bodyguard were surrounded by a detachment of Ethiopian
soldiers, one of whom recognized the Himyarite king and
smote him a deadly blow. According to some Muslim traditions, however, the king of the Himyarites, on finding himself about to be surrounded by his enemies, galloped through
their ranks toward the sea and, being hotly pursued by the
Ethiopians, he managed to escape capture only by driving
his horse over a high cliff and plunging into the foaming
Arabian sea. With victory thus assured, this southern Ara-

bian kingdom remained under Ethiopian rule for nearly a hundred years.

In addition to being one of the ablest of the early "Defenders of the Faith" on foreign soil, Caleb would seem, like Ezana, to have taken very active steps to promote the continued growth and spread of the Christian religion in his own land. In an early medieval document, it is reported that after the Axumite king's victory over the enemies of the Southern Arabian Christians, he sent ambassadors to Alexandria with a message to Justinian requesting that men learned in the Christian faith be sent to him for the purpose of spreading further the teachings of Christ among the subjects of his empire. Justinian, in response to this request, ordered Licinius, his viceroy in Alexandria, to assist the ambassadors in finding the type of men capable of carrying on the evangelical work which the Ethiopian king desired. The emissaries chose Bishop John, the Almoner of the Church of St. John in Alexandria—"a good and pious man of about sixty-two years of age"—as the leader of the projected enterprise, "along with several other holy men." The surviving records tell us nothing of the details of their labors; but there are preserved a number of general statements to the effect that Bishop John and his coworkers, on their arrival in Ethiopia, "baptized the king and a number of his courtiers and nobles," and that through their efforts "churches were erected in various parts of the Kingdom." With the support of such an able patron of the Church as King Caleb appears to have been, there are good reasons for believing that the efforts of Bishop John and the "holy men" who assisted him were indeed no less fruitful than had been the harvest reaped by Frumentius and his coadjutors in the Ethiopian "vineyard of the Lord."

In 533 Justinian, then at the height of his power as emperor of the Byzantine Empire, sent a diplomatic mission, headed by Nonnosus, to Axum to secure Caleb's cooperation in an economic and a military alliance against the Persian King Chosroes I.

Justinian's objectives in promoting this alliance were three-fold: the first, economic; the second, military; and the third, religious in character. With reference to the first of these objectives, Procopius, to whom we are indebted for much knowledge of this matter, states that it was Justinian's plan to have the Ethiopians replace the Persians as the middlemen through whom the merchants of the Byzantine empire would procure the silks and other products of the East. With the Ethiopians and their subjects in southern Arabia serving as the chief brokers for this extensive trade, Justinian hoped to secure a monopoly for the Byzantine merchants in the west, and thus free the inhabitants of the Roman Empire of "the necessity of having to do business with their enemies." The second objective was to have the Ethiopians and their vassal states in southwestern Arabia join Byzantium in a concerted attack on Persia, for it is true that despite the "Everlasting Peace" which Justinian had made with Chosroes in 532, with the purpose of freeing the imperial armies for operations in Italy and northern Africa, Justinian knew well that the peace was but a truce and that before long the two empires would again be locked in mortal combat.

Justinian's third objective was to strengthen and unify the Christian world in such a manner that would enable it to resist the forces of the idolatrous and pagan nations by which it was so largely surrounded. Since the Christian kingdoms of Ethiopia were the only other independent Christian powers in the world at that time, it is understandable enough that Justinian should have sought their cooperation in this ambitious enterprise.

Some modern historians have often observed that if the provisions and intentions of the alliance between Justinian and the Ethiopian king could have been realized, the subsequent history of the whole world might have been vastly different from what it turned out to be. But Justinian's planned New Order for the world was not realized. The part of the plan that envisioned the Persians being replaced by the Ethiopians as the chief middlemen in the trade with the East, went awry, as Procopius points out, because the Persian merchants, being neighbors of the Indians and numerous in the ports first reached by Indian ships, adopted the practice of buying up all or most of the silks and other products of the east, thus leaving nothing or very little for the Ethiopians to purchase.

The provisions of the military alliance were upset by Persia. Chosroes, alarmed by Justinian's successes in Italy and northern Africa, and angered no doubt also by the knowledge of the Byzantine emperor's alliance with the Ethiopians, broke the provisions of the truce, invaded, and overran Justinian's eastern provinces, while Justinian's hands were tied by the demands of his campaigns in the West. As a consequence, Justinian was forced to sue for and accept a disadvantageous peace which weakened considerably Byzantium's position in the East. In the meantime, the Byzantine Empire was further weakened by the ravages of a very severe and disastrous epidemic of the bubonic plague which killed millions of Justinian's subjects.

Under these circumstances it is hardly necessary to say that neither Justinian nor his successor was in any position to implement the provisions of Byzantium's alliance with the Ethiopians. In 542 King Caleb, with whom the alliance had been made, voluntarily "retired from the world," and became a humble monk in order that he might devote his declining years entirely to study of the "divine word" of the "Perfect One" whose cause, in younger years, he had striven so ably to serve. Caleb was succeeded first by his eldest son, Beta Israel, and next by his second son, Gabra Maskal— whose name meant "Servant of the Cross." Few particulars have survived of the reign of the first of the princes, but there is much information available on Gabra Maskal's reign and all of this shows that he was, like his father, an able prince and a devout patron of the church. The kingdom is said to have been exceptionally prosperous in his reign and it is reported that it was he who sent to Abreha, the Ethiopian viceroy in Arabia, the gold and silver and precious stones, as well as the artificers, employed by Abreha in building his magnificent church. Maskal is also credited with having built and endowed a number of churches in his native land itself.

Having overrun Byzantium's eastern provinces, Chosroes, a few years later, turned his forces against Ethiopia's vassal states in southwestern Arabia. By winning the non-Christian Arabs to his side, he succeeded in smashing completely Ethiopian dominion in that area. The Persians then held the country as overlords until their power was broken less than a century later by the Islamized Arabs.

While it is true that the Persian conquest and domination of southwestern Arabia did not destroy Christianity in the region, the new religion did lose much of the vigor and vitality that had characterized it under the protection and government of the Ethiopians. Edward Gibbon, in summing up the consequences of the expulsion of the Ethiopians from the peninsula, has observed that "if a Christian power had been maintained in Arabia, Mohammed must have been crushed in his cradle, and Abyssinia would have prevented a revolution which has changed the civil and religious state of the world."

Gibbon notes that Justinian had been reproached for his alliance with the Ethiopians but, in the light of the preceding observations, it would appear that there was more statesmanship embodied in this act than the Byzantine emperor was himself, perhaps, able to discern. It is hardly to be doubted that had Justinian and his immediate successors been in the position to have implemented more effectively the military schemes which gave rise to the alliance, the Ethiopians would have been both willing and able to have carried through their part of the bargain. But the Ethiopians were engaged in their contests with Arabs and the Persians; and Byzantium, instead of being able to fight on the offensive, was engaged in one of the most trying defensive struggles in the empire's entire history. Had the situation been otherwise, there are good reasons for believing that the Ethiopians would have succeeded in maintaining their political supremacy in Arabia for some time to come; and, in that event, it is very probable that the "Flame of Islam," as Gibbon and others have observed, would indeed have been extinguished forever in the initial clashes between the Champions of the Crescent and the Soldiers of the Cross.

The campaigns in southern Arabia and the alliance with Byzantium signalized Ethiopia's full emergence as a great Christian state which was second to none in wealth, influence, and dedication to the Christian faith among the great powers of the age.*

---

* One should note that in the process of establishing Christianity as the state religion and Ethiopia as one of the world champions of the faith, the monarchy became the supreme protector of the Ethiopian Church. At the same time the monarchy, by making tax-exempt, non-reappropriative land grants to the church, assured that the latter would become a powerful social, economic and political force in Ethiopia. It is this marriage of the monarchy and Christianty which formed the principal institutional pillar in Ethiopian history.

IV

Prester John and Diplomatic Correspondence with European Powers

The legend of Prester John rivals that of the Queen of Sheba both in ubiquity and in impact. For centuries European merchants, travelers, missionaries, and statesmen speculated on the location of the "rich and powerful" Prester John, placing him and his kingdom first someplace in Asia, and finally in Africa. Rumor had it that he was a powerful Christian monarch whose armies had dealt successfully with the Muslims. Over the years, therefore, Christian rulers in Europe envisioned an alliance with Prester John to combat their common Muslim foe. The drama which surrounded these rumors and speculations mounted as letters from Christian kings in Ethiopia appeared in Europe. All of these exciting episodes are discussed by Professor Hansberry in the following essay.

This particular essay supports the general theme of emerging Ethiopian identity and unity by showing how the Prester John legend, and both diplomatic and religious correspondence and the exchange of emissaries between Ethiopia and Europe, contributed to the solidification of a national image of Ethiopia in the international arena; while at

110

the same time, Ethiopian rulers were responding as a national entity to the several opportunities provided by the world powers. In short, in addition to the unifying character of the monarchy and the church, both of which directly affected all Ethiopians, developments on the world scene required that the Ethiopian ruling elite define their constituency. Indeed, these internal and external factors reinforced each other to form the nationalizing threads which enabled the country to stand independent of alien rule, except for the brief interregnum of Italian occupation, 1935–41.

The Editor

In the middle and later centuries of the Middle Ages, Europe repeatedly extended itself in a series of efforts to repel a succession of assaults on the ramparts of Christendom in the east. The Seljuk Turks made devastating inroads into the eastern provinces of the Byzantine Empire in the eleventh century; and in the twelfth and thirteenth, Saladin and his Mameluk successors eventually broke the power of the European crusaders in Palestine and Syria. While the Christians from the west were still engaged in these terrific conflicts with the Muslim infidels of the East, there appeared an even more terrifying enemy which threatened to outdo the attacks of the Crescent upon the Cross. The pagan Mongols under Genghis Khan and his successors, after having subdued most of central and western Asia, were sweeping over eastern and central Europe with a fury which seemed to know no bounds. Like a mighty tide, the Golden Horde overwhelmed much of Russia, Poland, and Hungary, and for a time it appeared as if all Europe would be inundated by the onrushing Mongol flood. The impact of these pagan eruptions and infidel attacks upon Christendom caused medieval Europe to quake to its very foundations; fear and terror were everywhere.

While these several developments were straining the courage and faith of many Europeans, there sprang up on the continent a rumor which did more to revive national and Christian hope than any amount of pious appeal alone would ever have been able to accomplish. This rumor was to the effect that in the distant east there was a mighty Christian potentate named Prester John who had broken the power of the Muslim infidels and was slaughtering the Mongols like lambs. But more important than this, so the rumor went, this mighty Christian prince had announced that he was ready and willing to form a compact with the European Christians and join them in their holy war against their hated foes. This rumor flew from mouth to mouth and from land to land and soon crystalized into an almost universal belief which brought boundless hope to the desponding and be-leaguered Christian world.

Exactly how, when, and where this rumor began no one in Europe seemed to know; nor was there, for a very long time, any one on the continent who could say for a certainty where Prester John's empire was situated or how it could be reached. Some thought that it was hidden away in the far recesses of central Asia or northern India, but others main-tained that it was composed of a number of African king-doms lying beyond the western shores of the Indian Ocean and the Red Sea.

If the problem of the origin of the rumor about Prester John and the question of his identity and the situation of his empire were matters which seriously divided European opinion in the Middle Ages, the same has been no less true in geographical and historical circles of our own times. Some modern scholars, like their medieval predecessors, are of the opinion that the rumor originated from European echoes of the existence of some Nestorian Christian kingdom in central Asia and the name Prester John is supposed to have been the corrupt or misunderstood form of the title of its king. Those who advocate this view think that about a century or more after the origin of the rumor about Prester John, the title which had been formerly applied to the Nestorian potentate in Asia was transferred to the Christian king of Ethiopia.

Other students of these questions reject this point of view. They point out, as we shall presently see, that despite the several known attempts that were made in the twelfth and thirteenth centuries to establish contacts with Prester John by searching for him in Asia, no Christian prince or Christian state which fitted the prevailing descriptions of him and his empire was ever found. Those who take this position believe that the rumors and traditions about Prester John and his empire must have referred, from the very be-ginning, to what were in reality the kings of the Christian kingdom of Ethiopia. As there was no comparable Christian

potentate or Christian state in Asia which could have provided such a basis, it is insisted that the rumors and traditions must have been founded upon bits of genuine information about the real Christian kings and the real Christian
states which are now known to have been flourishing in
Ethiopia at that period. It may be observed that the evidence relating to the state of affairs in Ethiopia, Europe, and
Asia in the twelfth, thirteenth, and fourteenth centuries,
would seem on the whole to favor the latter point of view.
There is an abundance of evidence which shows that the
kings and kingdoms of Ethiopia and Nubia in the twelfth
and thirteenth centuries might well have served as the pro-
totypes of the potentate Prester John and the empire over
which he was said by European rumor to rule. Not only was
Christianity the state religion of these kingdoms but their
kings were priests as the European rumor affirmed.

There is even some evidence which indicates that the
name John (Latin, *Johannes*) in the title, Prester John, was
only a corruption of the Ethiopian word *Zan*. As there are
known to have been numerous pilgrims from European and
Ethiopian lands in Palestine at this very period, and as the
records indicate that there were intimate associations between the representatives of these widely sundered regions
of Christendom, there was ample opportunity for an exchange of information about their respective countries. In
this way the particulars just mentioned about the kings and
kingdoms of Ethiopia and Nubia might well have been carried back to Europe where they gave rise to the rumors and
traditions about Prester John. It is true that a number of the
earliest surviving records, in which references to Prester
John occur, leave no doubt of the fact that their authors
were of the opinion that the priest-king and his empire were
situated in Asia; but this might well have been due, in part
at least, to the chaotic state of geographical knowledge in
Europe at that period.

Whatever may have been the real origin of the medieval

rumors and traditions about Prester John, it is generally agreed that from the first quarter of the fourteenth century onward, most of the references and allusions to him placed the mysterious monarch and his empire in Ethiopia.* How the early uncertainty about his continental situation affected the course of historical events in Europe in the late Middle Ages and how the kings of Ethiopia came finally to be universally identified with the eagerly sought potentate will be made clear in the following review of the efforts that were made to establish contact with him.

From the very beginning of the rumor to the effect that in the East somewhere there was a mighty Christian prince named Prester John who was waging successful warfare against the pagan Mongols and the Muslim infidels, there were those who counseled that emissaries should be dispatched to the Levant for the purpose of searching out this mighty monarch with the view of sealing with him a compact that would secure his aid in the holy war against the enemies of the faith. While such an undertaking was under deliberation, western Christendom was stirred by the announcement that Manuel Comnenus, Emperor of the Byzantine Empire, had received in person a long letter from the great potentate. Some critics believe that similar letters were also received by Pope Alexander III; by Frederic Barbarossa, Emperor of the Holy Roman Empire; by Louis VII of France; and by Alfonso Henrique, King of Portugal. Unfortunately, the original manuscript of none of these letters was preserved, but what are alleged to be copies of certain of them have come down to us in a considerable number.

---

* In 1306 Prester John is alleged to have sent 30 envoys to the King of Spain with an offer of aid against "infidels." The envoys also visited Pope Clement V at Avignon and the churches of Peter and Paul in Rome. Thirty-three years later (1339) the earliest known map to place Prester John in Ethiopia was made in Mallorca. (See O. G. S. Crawford, *Ethiopian Itineraries*, Cambridge University Press, 1958, p. 5.)

It is reported that there are eight manuscript copies in the British Museum, ten in Vienna, thirteen in Paris and fifteen in Munich. According to the medieval Chronicle of Albericus Trium Fontium, the letter to the Byzantine emperor was received in 1165. The letters as they are known from their alleged copies are most extraordinary documents. Elsewhere in this essay will be found lengthy excerpts—along with critical comments on a number of passages—from a copy of the letter addressed to Emperor Manuel, but a few observations indicating its general character may be noted at this point.

The letter opens with the salutation "John, Priest of the Almighty Power of God and the Strength of Our Lord Jesus Christ, King of Kings and Lord of Lords to his friend Emmanuel, Prince of Constantinople—greetings and best wishes for his health, prosperity, and his continuance in Divine Favor." From its context the letter would appear to have had a four-fold purpose. The first was to thank the prince of Constantinople for the love and good will which he was reported to entertain for his distant brother in the faith, for the letter states that "we have been informed that news of our greatness has reached you and that you hold us in high esteem." The distant prince also wished to thank the Byzantine emperor for "some treasures of art and other objects of interest" which he had sent—or, according to some translations, had "expressed the desire" to send—to him. In response to this kindness, so the letter observes, "we have instructed our treasurer to send you some of our own objects of art." The second purpose was to solicit from the prince of Constantinople a true report concerning his religious practices and beliefs for, the letter states, "rumor has reached us that your court regards you as a god, though we know that you are mortal and subject to the infirmities common to mankind," and therefore "we desire to be made certain that you hold the right faith and in all things cleave to Our Lord Jesus Christ." The third objective of the royal letter writer was to announce his intention to visit the Holy Sepulcher at Jerusalem and to offer his services in the campaign "to humble and chastise the enemies of the Cross." And finally, the fourth purpose of the letter was to convey a true report of the greatness and excellency of the vast dominions under his rule: "Let it be known and believed that I, Prester John, Lord of Lords, surpass all other princes under heaven in virtue, in riches, and in power." The letter then proceeds to give an extended account of the size, wealth, and organization of his empire, as well as a lengthy review of the manner in which the principles and precepts of the Christian religion were preached and practiced in his land.

For about two decades prior to the receipt of this letter, the trend of affairs had been particularly unfavorable to the crusaders and the Byzantine Greeks in the east. In 1144, the Latin principality of Edessa had fallen before the attacks launched by the Seljuks to push with vigor the war against the Christians in Syria. The Second Crusade (1147–1149) under Louis VII of France and Conrad III of the Holy Roman Empire had proved a miserable fiasco, while Arslan II, the Seljuk Sultan of Iconium, had been successful in consolidating and expanding his power in Anatolia, largely at the expense of Byzantium. It is therefore not difficult to believe, as tradition avers, that the announcement of the arrival of Prester John to the Byzantine emperor and the other European princes was hailed with hope and joy throughout Christian Europe. For centuries, so far as the evidence indicates, no one seems ever to have questioned the genuineness of these letters and in the course of time there grew up around them and their contents a vast literature, a fact which is reflected in the large number of copies of the letters that have survived to the present day. They were included in, or alluded to, many of the chronicles and romances of the time, and parts of them or matters about which they spoke were turned into rhyme and sung all over Europe by minstrels and troubadours.

But if the Europeans of the Middle Ages—learned and laity alike—accepted the letters at their face value, several modern scholars are far from being convinced that the famous epistles are what they are purported to have been. Many scholars, among them some of the most eminent students of the Prester John tradition, have gone so far as to contend that the letters were rank forgeries. Instead of having been fashioned in the chancellery of Prester John, as their texts imply, these critics are generally disposed to think that the letters were fabricated by some priestly puck. Father Christian, the Archbishop of Mainz, is charged with having been the author of one allegedly fraudulent letter, solely on the grounds that he is said to have translated from Greek into Latin the letter addressed to the Emperor Frederick Barbarossa. It is supposed that the archbishop perpetrated the fraud to aid the cause of his emperor, who was at the time engaged in a bitter controversy with Pope Alexander III. Other scholars, however, have suggested that the letters were probably written by some Nestorian monk or priest in the Levant and then dispatched to the west with the hope of inspiring European Christendom to renewed courage in its contest with the eastern enemies of the church.

Despite their wide acceptance, none of these attempts to explain away the genuineness of the letters can be regarded as more than interesting and ingenious, or perhaps noningenious, suggestions. For, as has been intimated, there is no scrap of positive evidence upon which these suggestions rest. The disposition on the part of modern scholars to question or to reject the authenticity of the letters is founded primarily upon inferences and conclusions arrived at on the basis of critical examinations of the texts of the letters themselves. In their examination of the available texts, some critics have made much of the fact that a number of the passages refer to matters and events which could have had but little if any relationship to reality. It is contended that some of the claims presented in these passages are so obviously and entirely fabulous that they could have had no basis in fact whatsoever. On the strength of these considerations it is concluded that the letters must have been bare fabrications from start to finish.

It is admittedly true that in copies of the letters that have been preserved, there are numerous statements which are difficult to accept at face value, and there are certainly some passages which are entirely of an apocryphal character. It is also a fact that the general overtones of the letters as a whole have something of a fabulous ring about them. In making these admissions, however, it needs to be borne in mind that none of the original manuscripts of these letters has come down to us; hence, there is no way of knowing how closely the available copies follow the texts of the original manuscripts. It is entirely possible that many of the admittedly apocryphal passages are the result of interpolations and attempted emendations by the medieval editors and translators to whom we are indebted for the surviving copies of the original texts. The fact that purported copies of the same letter often differ in details tends to lend a certain measure of support to this suggestion. It is also true that despite the fabulous character of certain passages in their texts, the letters contain many statements which not only have the ring of truth, but which can be verified as being in substantial accord with historical fact. Particularly is this true if these statements are examined in the light of the now available evidence regarding the political, cultural, and religious history of Ethiopia during the age from which the letters under consideration date.

The letter to Emperor Manuel was received in the year 1165. At that time Ethiopia was being ruled by what is commonly known as the Zagwe dynasty. The last and the best known king of this dynasty was the celebrated Lalibela, who is regarded by native tradition as one of the greatest and most saintly rulers in the history of the country. The famous rock-hewn churches of Lasta are generally attributed by native tradition and modern scholars to this king (as mentioned in Chapter IV). The sovereign who erected these churches must have had enormous resources at his command and it is generally agreed that he was not only zealous in the faith and a great patron of the church, but in all respects an extraordinary prince. The dates of Lalibela's reign can not now be exactly determined; but the indications are that his rule covered much of the last half of the twelfth century and it is quite probable that he was on the throne in 1165. In a still extant story of his life, said to have been written for the Ethiopian monastery of Golgotha—presumably the one in Jerusalem—it is reported that before becoming king, Lalibela visited the holy places in the Holy Land; and although some of the details recorded in the account are admittedly apocryphal, there is no reason to doubt that the reported pilgrimage did occur. In the accounts of his life available to us, no mention is made of a subsequent journey to Jerusalem, but it is hardly likely that so zealous a prince would have neglected to perform the sacred pilgrimage after he ascended the throne. But if he did not revisit—or even visit at all—the Holy Land, there is every probability that Lalibela was reasonably well informed not only about the main course of political and religious affairs in Palestine, but in Christian Europe as well. For it will be recalled that Jerusalem and the neighboring areas were at that time still in the Crusaders' hands; hence, information concerning affairs in the west, including the names of the leading European rulers of the day, might well have been acquired by the Ethiopian pilgrims to the Holy Land and carried back by them to their own king and country. It will also be remembered that the letter addressed to the "Prince of Constantinople" clearly implies that the Byzantine emperor had previously sent greetings and gifts to Prester John, and it is indicated that the latter's letter was an acknowledgment and reply in kind. Just as the Ethiopians could have learned of affairs in the Christian west through the European pilgrims and crusaders in Palestine, so could the latter have acquired information about Christian Ethiopia and its king.

Having been informed of these matters by returning pilgrims, nothing would have been more natural than that Emmanuel should have sent greetings and gifts by way of Jerusalem to this potential African ally; nor is there any reason the Ethiopian prince could not have sent his reply over the same route by which the Byzantine emperor's message had arrived. Despite their admittedly fabulous passages—which may well have been interpolations—the letters of 1165 also contain several allusions to, or reasonably accurate descriptions of, many court and religious practices, as well as political and geographical conditions, that are now known to have prevailed in Ethiopia in the Middle Ages. Parts of these letters are also remarkably similar in style and spirit to letters which were sent to European princes and popes by Ethiopian kings in later times and about which no question of authenticity has been raised. Even the pharaseology in the two groups of letters is often practically identical. If the letters of 1165 were fabricated, their fraudulent author or authors must have been in possession of a considerable amount of genuine information about the Christian kingdom of Ethiopia at that period. But in the light of the preceding discussion there would seem to be no real reason the original letters could not have been essentially what their contents asserted them to be.

In 1177 another message, said to have been from Prester John, arrived in Europe and was received with scarcely less acclaim than was the letter of 1165. Most modern scholars agree that this message was in all likelihood what it was purported to be and had been sent at the insistence of a Christian potentate whose kingdom was situated somewhere in the east. The message was addressed to Pope Alexander III and was brought to Rome by one Master Philip, who is said to have been the private physician and the confidential adviser of the pope. How and where the physician Philip acquired this message is not known. Modern scholars who lean to the view that the earliest notices concerning Prester John referred to a potentate in Asia, think it probable that Philip had traveled in the Far East and had received the message from some Christian king of that region. On the other hand, scholars who are of the opinion that the Christian king of Ethiopia provided, from the beginning, the real basis for the origin of the Prester John tradition, have attributed the message to an Ethiopian king; and it is supposed that it was delivered to Philip through Ethiopian intermediaries whom he met in Jerusalem in the course of a pilgrimage to the Holy Land. Whether the message was a written or oral communication is also not clear, but it would appear to have been oral. Most of the Christians of the east at that period were Nestorians, Monophysites, or Jacobites and were regarded as heretics by the Christians of the west. Prester John would seem to have been rather much concerned about these schismatic differences and their disruptive effects upon the unity of the Church. The removal of these differences would seem to have been a main objective of Prester John's message, for in the reports that have come down to us, it is stated that he desired to become better acquainted with the doctrines and disciplines of the Catholic Church and was eager to heal the breach that separated him and his people from their European brothers in the faith. The message also disclosed that he was eager to build or acquire a Church—or possibly a hospice or monastery, presumably for his own people—in the city of Rome.

Pope Alexander III replied to these requests in a long and interesting letter of which several copies are available to us. Manuscript copies are preserved in the library of Cambridge University and in the Bibliothèque nationale, and notices of it are also to be found in several chronicles surviving from medieval times. The letter bears the date September 27, 1177, and appears to have been written while the pope was in Venice where he had gone for an important meeting with the German Emperor Frederick Barbarossa. The pope's letter is addressed to "Our Most Dear Son in Christ, the Illustrious and Magnificent King of the Indians and the Most Holy of Priests." (Ethiopia in the Middle Ages, as well as in ancient times, was frequently called India and its inhabitants were often designated as the Indi or the Indians of Africa.) The pope explains in the opening paragraph that he had heard, through common report and from manifold narrators, of the king's Christian profession and his "piety and diligence in good works." He then refers specifically to the monarch's special requests, and states that these had reached him through his physician, Master Philip, who had, in the course of his travels, "met and conferred with honorable persons" from the priest-king's empire. Because of the remote location of the monarch's realm, it was considered impossible to send a papal legate to his distant court; but the pope signified that he would give careful and sympathetic consideration to the king's special requests.

The Pope admonished his "Most Dear Son in Christ" that "the more nobly and magnanimously thou conductest thyself and the less thou vauntest of thy wealth and power, the more readily shall we be disposed to grant thy wishes. . . ." Whether this admonition was inspired by some boastful remark in the messages delivered by Master Philip, or whether it was provoked by the passage in the letter of 1165 in which Prester John had declared that he surpassed "all princes under heaven in virtue, riches, and power," is a question to which the available sources do not provide a satisfactory answer. If we could be sure, and it seems most likely, that the latter remark was responsible for the rebuke, it would be necessary to conclude that both Pope Alexander and his physician, Master Philip, were of the opinion that the letter of 1165 and the message of 1177 were from the same potentate. This would indicate that neither the pope nor his advisers had any doubt about the genuineness of either of the messages. Had the first letter been a mere priestly invention, as some supposed, it is possible but hardly probable that the secret could have been so well kept that the papal court would have remained in complete ignorance of the letter's fraudulent origin from 1165 to 1177. But it is reasonable to suppose that during this period, enough of the secret would have leaked out to have made the pope and his advisers at least suspicious about its authenticity. Had there been any cause whatsoever to doubt the genuineness of the letter of 1165, it is difficult to believe that the pope would not have been hesitant about accepting the message of 1177 at its face value. But there is no evidence that he or anyone else of his time entertained the slightest doubt about the genuineness of the latter message—in fact everything suggests that he was absolutely convinced of its authenticity. That this was so, together with the fact that the papal rebuke to Prester John would seem to have been inspired by the beautiful passage in the letter of 1165, makes it reasonably certain that the pope not only regarded both messages as genuine but considered them to have been from the same king. And as has been previously indicated, there are no legitimate grounds for doubting that such was indeed the fact.

After his tempered rebuke, the pope closed his letter with the request that the priest-king send to him "honorable men with letters sealed with thy seal and in which thy request shall be set forth at length." The task of delivering the letter was entrusted to Master Philip who in due course set out again for the east. The available records relating to the letter of 1177 do not carry us beyond this point in the story. This being so, we do not know whether the letter did or did not reach its intended destination. It is very probable, however, that it did, for the letter would need to have been carried by Philip only as far as Jerusalem where it could have been turned over to the Abbot of the Ethiopian monastery or to the keepers of the Ethiopian Chapel in Jerusalem who would have dispatched it to their king by Ethiopian pilgrims returning to their own country. We have seen that, among other things, Prester John was eager to have a church or a college at Rome and it is an interesting fact that the Ethiopians of a later period did own, and maintain for some time, a church in the Italian city. This church was situated in back of the apse of St. Peter's Cathedral. The date and the circumstances under which the Ethiopians acquired this church are not known; some have thought that it was probably assigned to them through the negotiations of the Ethiopian delegates to the Council of Florence (1439–1441); but Cardinal Baronius (1538–1607) suggested that it may have been granted to the Ethiopians as early as the time of Pope Alexander III and in direct response to Prester John's request as set forth in his message of 1177.

If surviving medieval sources are to be believed, it would appear that correspondence between the popes of Rome and the kings of Ethiopia, as well as direct contacts between European and African kingdoms, were much more common in the thirteenth and fourteenth centuries than is usually supposed. In one of these medieval documents—a letter written by Nicolò Fortiguera to Pope Benedict XIII (1394–1423)—it is stated that Pope Innocent IV (1243–1254) sent a number of Dominican monks to Ethiopia. Certain bulls issued by Innocent IV also refer to this mission; and from the texts of these bulls it would seem that a similar mission was sent to the Christian kingdoms of Nubia during the same period. If the monarch to whom the message of 1177 was addressed was in reality an Ethiopian king, it is not improbable that the Dominican mission had been dispatched by Pope Innocent IV to Ethiopia as a part of a program to effect the reconciliation between that country and the Catholic Church as had been proposed by the king who had sent the message to Pope Alexander III. The king of Ethiopia during the pontificate of Innocent IV and therefore the sovereign of the country who would have received this mission was Naakueto Laab, who reigned from around

1228 to about 1268 or 1270. He was a nephew of the great Lalibela and is said to have been regarded, like his uncle, as a saint and a devoted patron of the church. It is reasonable to suppose, therefore, that the mission would have fared well at his hands.

It is also reported that letters were also sent to the kings of Ethiopia by Pope Alexander IV (1254–1261), Urban IV (1261–1265), Clement IV (1265–1268), Innocent V (1276), Nicholas III (1277–1280), Nicholas IV (1288–1294), Benedict XI (1303–1304), Clement V (1305–1314), and John XXII (1316–1334). It may be observed that although no copies of these papal letters would seem to have survived, it is possible to identify by name all of the Ethiopian kings to whom they must have been addressed. As Naakueto Laab remained on the throne until about 1268 or 1270, the letters of Alexander IV and Urban IV must have been sent to this prince and the same was probably true of the letter of Clement IV. Naakueto Laab was succeeded by Yekuno Amlak who reigned from about 1270 to about 1285. It is reported that he corresponded with Baybars I (1260–1277), the Mameluke Sultan of Egypt, and with the Byzantine Emperor Michael VIII Palaeologus (1261–1282) to whom he sent, among other things, several giraffes as gifts. It was to this king that the letters of Innocent V and Nicholas III must have been dispatched. It is significant that Theodosius II, the Patriarch of the Coptic Church in Alexandria and, by tradition, the nominal head of the Ethiopian Church, is said to have quarreled bitterly with Yekuno Amlak and to have been the source of much intrigue in the kingdom during that king's reign. There is but little doubt that these disturbances were caused, in part at least, by the Coptic patriarch's opposition to the increasingly friendly relationships between the Ethiopians and the popes of the Roman Catholic Church. The surviving copy of the letter of Pope Nicholas IV bears the date July 11, 1289. The king of Ethiopia at that period was Yagbea Seyon who reigned from about 1285 to 1294; and it was to this king that Pope Nicholas' letter must have been addressed.

What were the ways and means by which this letter, and the other papal communications mentioned, might have reached their intended destinations? When Saladin upset the rule of the Crusaders in Jerusalem and restored the city to the control of the Muslims in 1187, an agreement was worked out between Saladin's brother and the king of Ethiopia that guaranteed to the Ethiopians the continued possession of their monastery in the Holy City. This agreement seems still to have been in force when Yagbea Seyon came to the throne, for it is reported that he maintained direct communications with the Ethiopian monks in Jerusalem and sent them generous supplies. Saladin, it will be remembered, also guaranteed to European Christians the right to continue their pilgrimages to the Holy City. Through these arrangements the Christians of Europe and Ethiopia were able to continue their contacts with each other by way of Jerusalem. This would seem to show that a way was still open through which Pope Nicholas' letter and the other papal communications might have reached Ethiopia.

What was alleged to be a copy of a letter written by Nicholas IV has survived, though it does not mention the Ethiopian king by name. It is addressed, simply, to the *Imperatori Aethiopiae*. It is said to have been entrusted for delivery to the care of John de Monte Corvino, a Minorite friar who won distinction as a missionary in the Near East, India, and China between the years 1275 and 1333. As Friar John himself does not seem ever to have visited Ethiopia, it may be presumed that he was charged with conveying the letter from Rome to some point in the Near East—probably Jerusalem—where it was turned over to others who carried it to its final destination. The monks in the Ethiopian monastery of Jerusalem to whom King Yagbea Seyon is said to have sent supplies might well have been charged by Corvino with this responsibility.

That the letter from Nicholas IV would seem to have reached the Ethiopian king is indicated by the following interesting fact. In a letter written from his mission-station in

China in February 1306, Corvino mentions that he had recently been visited by "a solemn delegation from the land of Ethiopia" which had invited him to come and preach in their country. If he could not come himself, the Ethiopians requested that he send them "other good preachers" for the same purpose. The letter does not state whether this delegation was from Ethiopia or from some other Christian kingdom in the Sudan. In presenting their invitation, the members of the delegation mentioned in passing, however, that the Apostle Matthew and his disciples had preached in their country. Indeed, a number of ecclesiastical chronicles and other ancient and medieval records frequently state that Matthew, like Matthias and Bartholomew, had preached in Ethiopia but unfortunately none of these early records makes it clear whether "Ethiopia" means the Ethiopian kingdom, or the Sudan in general. The remark made to Corvino by the Ethiopian emissaries is therefore of little help in determining the exact identity of the country from which they came.

Although no copies of the letters reported to have been written by Benedict XI and Clement V seem to have survived, it is of interest to note that Wedem Arad, the king of Ethiopia during the time, is said to have sent a mission of thirty ambassadors to the papal court during this period. The mission is reported to have been received by Pope Clement V at Avignon in France, which was the seat of the Holy See from 1309 to 1377. The specific purpose of the envoys' visit is not known, but there is reason to suppose that their mission was associated in some way with the matters which must have been discussed in the letters said to have been sent by Pope Benedict and Pope Clement. It may also be supposed that theirs, like the mission to Corvino in China, was charged by the king with inviting the Roman Catholic Church to send teachers and preachers to his country.

This suggestion finds some support in the fact that in

1316 eight Dominican monks are said to have arrived in Ethiopia by way of Palestine, Egypt, and Nubia. These preached with success in Nubia, and especially in Ethiopia. According to Dominican annals, the monks converted many Ethiopians to the doctrine of the Roman Catholic Church and even enrolled a number of proselytes in the Dominican Order; among these being a prince of the royal family. About the same period—sometime between 1316 and 1334—Bartholomew of Tivoli, a Dominican monk, was consecrated Bishop of Dongola, the name of one of the two Christian kingdoms of Nilotic Sudan; but it would appear that his duties were later extended to include Ethiopia. Bishop Bartholomew made his way from Europe to Palestine, Egypt, and Nubia, accompanied by Florentius and Subiacus, brothers of his order who were probably to serve him as suffragan bishops or coadjutors. Conditions in the Nubian kingdom were then in a critical state.* Although the sovereign of the country, King Kudanbes, and the majority of the inhabitants were Christians, large numbers of Muslims had been flocking into the kingdom ever since the Mameluke invasion in 1272–1275. Tensions between the adherents to the two religions had been steadily mounting and around 1325 broke out in the form of a bitter religious and dynastic war which culminated during the next two or three decades in the overthrow of Christianity and the complete destruction of the kingdom. In the midst of these distractions Bishop Bartholomew would seem to have fled to Ethiopia where he continued his labors with very fruitful results. The Dominican Order reported that he won many converts, including members of the nobility and the royal family. He is also said to have founded in Ethiopia a Dominican monastery, which added a number of distinguished Ethiopian recruits to the order.

These events occurred during the pontificate of Pope

---

* This visit by Bartholomew of Tivoli is still the subject of debate.

John XXII who, it will be remembered, is numbered among the pontiffs that are said to have written letters to the kings of Ethiopia. A copy of one of his letters has been preserved and bears the date September 11, 1329. Although that occurred during the reign of John XXII, the exact date Bishop Bartholomew went to Ethiopia is not known; but it could have been in or shortly after 1329, and it may have been he who delivered the pope's letter to the Ethiopian king. The sovereign of Ethiopia during this period was the celebrated Amda Tseyon I (1314–1344), son and successor of King Wedem Ared, and one of the ablest kings in the history of the country.

Wedem Ared's Muslim subjects had been encouraged and abetted in their budding disloyalty by their coreligionists in Arabia, Palestine, Syria, and Egypt. It has been suggested that the mission sent by Wedem Ared to Pope Clement V at Avignon may have been inspired by the desire to strengthen ties with the Christians of Europe as an offset to those ominous developments. In any case, shortly after Amda Tseyon ascended the throne, his Muslim subjects of the coastal regions broke into open rebellion and forced the king to react with a heavy hand. In the reigns of his immediate successors these rebellious activities were resumed, and grew in intensity as the centuries passed. They lasted for a period of over three hundred years and cost the country much in treasure and in lives.

These wars, together with the collapse of the Christian kingdoms of the eastern Sudan, and the intensification of the hatred between Muslims and Christians in Egypt and the Near East, tended to reduce greatly the contacts between Ethiopia and the outside world, including Christian Europe, for nearly two hundred years (from about 1330–1340 to about 1520–1530). Following the discovery and establishment of the ocean route to India and the east by the Portuguese in the late fifteenth and early sixteenth centuries, contacts between the Christian world and Ethiopia were resumed on a large scale; but even during the preceding two hundred years these relationships, though seriously curtailed, never completely ceased. Curiously enough, it was during this period of reduced contacts that the king of Ethiopia, rather than phantom Asian princes, came to be identified with the celebrated Prester John. The following is an account of these parallel if rather paradoxical developments.

In 1338 a group of thirty Dominican monks bearing passports and letters from the king of France set out for Ethiopia. They were intended, no doubt, to reinforce the Dominican mission which had been established in the country by Bishop Bartholomew. When they arrived in Egypt they presented their passports to the Muslim sultan, but instead of granting them safe conduct through his dominions he promptly and ruthlessly expelled them from his country. What happened to them after that is not known, but it is reasonably certain that they never reached their destination. Probably the growing bitterness between the Muslims and Christians influenced the sultan's attitude in this matter.

Between 1322 and 1327 the Byzantine emperor and Pope John XXII sent deputations to the sultan of Egypt to plead the cause of the Christians in that country. An appeal of the same character was also dispatched to Egypt by the Ethiopian King Amda Tseyon, warning the sultan that unless the repressive measures being imposed on the Egyptian Christians were revoked, he would institute a similar program of proscriptions against the Muslims in Ethiopia. In addition, the Ethiopian king threatened to divert the course of the Nile, which would have had the effect of transforming much of Egypt into a desert. It is known that threats of this type, in the earlier centuries of the Middle Ages, had more than once brought fear to the sultans of Egypt and forced them to be more charitable in their dealings with their Christian subjects. Whatever might have been the immediate effects of the appeals by the Byzantine emperor and the pope and the threatening warnings from the Ethiopian king, none of them would appear to have produced any lasting results. For in the reign of Newaya Krestos (1344–1372), the son and successor of Amda Tseyon, news arrived in Ethiopia that Abba Mark, the patriarch of Alexandria and the head of the Coptic Church, had been thrown into prison by order of the sultan, who was grievously taxing and otherwise persecuting the Egyptian Christians. On hearing this, Newaya Krestos renewed his father's threats and prepared to carry out the provisions with such effectiveness that the Egyptian sultan not only freed the patriarch but also abrogated his harsh measures against his Christian subjects.

A number of events and developments occurred and paved the way for the general acceptance of the Prester John identification. When the earliest information about Prester John began to echo through Europe, there was no certainty in the continent concerning the exact location of his empire. There is nothing in Pope Alexander III's reply to the message of 1177 to indicate whether he thought he was writing to an Asian or an African king, but it is generally agreed that Pope Nicholas IV and Pope John XXII knew very well that the empire of the potentate to whom their letters were addressed was situated in Africa. The statement of Nicolò Fortiguera to Pope Benedict XIII clearly implies that all of the other pontiffs mentioned in the same connection were quite aware of the fact that they were writing to an African king. It is obvious that both the Byzantine Emperor Michael VIII, Palaeologus, and Pope Clement V, who are reported to have entertained Ethiopian missions, knew very well that these were from Africa rather than Asia. Whether the Byzantine emperor and the several popes just mentioned did or did not identify these African kings with Prester John is not altogether clear; however, it is reasonable to suppose that at least they were inclined towards such an identification, but even this still was short of an exact location.

About this same period there began to circulate widely throughout Europe a popular tradition which did much to hasten the universal acceptance of the notion that Africa, rather than Asia, was the seat of the empire of Prester John. Such a tradition had evolved at least since Astolpho of England, an illustrious Christian knight living in the time of Charlemagne. Astolpho had paid a visit to a mighty Christian kingdom which was situated in "that part of Africa where the great River Nile has its source." This kingdom, so the tradition held, was ruled at the time by a potentate named Senapus who was supposed to have been one of the wealthiest and most powerful princes on all the earth. The palace of this prince was "one of surpassing splendor," and excelled in magnificence any palace in Europe. The bars and hinges and locks of its gates were "all of pure gold." Its columns were of rock crystal and its walls and ceilings were adorned with ornamental designs traced out in "rubies, emeralds, sapphires, and pearls." Indeed, it is related that gold was so abundant in the country that it was used in much the same way as other people employed iron. The land abounded in numerous plants that yielded sweetsmelling balms. The power of the king was said to be so great that the sultan of Egypt was wont to pay him annually a vast tribute, lest the monarch Senapus divert the course of the Nile and thereby "deprive Egypt of the source of its fertility."

When Astolpho departed the kingdom, Senapus allegedly sent with him an army of one hundred thousand men to assist Charlemagne and the Christians of Europe in their war against the Muslim infidels. The Saracens having been overwhelmed in a series of terrible battles, Astolpho took leave of his African legions and, after loading them down with spoil for themselves and gifts for their king, sent them back to their own land. This story survived in that celebrated collection of medieval legends, known as the Chansons de Gestes, from the eleventh century onward, and was almost universally attributed to the editorship of the Archbishop Turpin of Rheims who was, like Astolpho, one of Charlemagne's twelve most illustrious knights. Modern historians of French literature are on the whole, however, of the opinion that Archbishop Turpin had nothing to do with these stories. It is now generally supposed that these tales were first put into literary form by monks in the eleventh and twelfth centuries and that they unscrupulously credited their efforts to the renowned archbishop with the view of winning a larger audience than their own literary reputation could command. Those who take this position feel that Astolpho's alleged visit and adventures had no foundation in fact; but whether this is true or not, the tale was widely known and, apparently, widely believed at the time when the story of Prester John first began to sweep Europe. Although Senapus, the distant Christian king whom Astolpho is alleged to have visited, is not identified as Prester John in the literary accounts available to us, the details and the spirit of the two stories parallel each other rather closely at a number of points. The potentates described in each were not only very powerful and rich but both were inveterate foes of the infidel enemies of the Christian faith. As the two stories circulated simultaneously throughout much of Europe, they must often have been blended and fused into one tradition by the popular mind. The vagueness about the geographical position of Prester John's empire, together with the fact that the kingdom of Senapus was definitely stated to be "in that part of Africa where the great River Nile has its source," indicate that there must have been an ever increasing number of persons disposed to place the priest-king's lordly domains in Africa rather than Asia.

In the latter part of the thirteenth and the first part of the fourteenth centuries, even more definite evidence began to appear in support of an African location of Prester John's empire. In 1245, or a hundred years after the first of all known written accounts—that of Otto of Freisingen—referring to Prester John appeared, Pope Innocent IV sent a mission into central Asia which, along with other duties, was charged to be on the alert for information about the location of Prester John's empire. This mission, headed by Giovanni de Piano Carpini, an Italian and a Franciscan friar, penetrated as far east as the capital of the Great Khan, deep in the heart of Mongolia, and returned to Europe in the autumn of 1247. In a report written of his remarkable journey—the first ever to reach so far to the east—Carpini narrated at considerable length his manifold observations and experiences, but of Prester John and his empire he saw absolutely nothing and only heard a few vague rumors to the effect that some years before a Christian prince of that name, living in Greater India had overwhelmed a great Tartar army by the aid of Greek Fire. He mentioned having heard echoes of a black race who dwelt somewhere in the East and who were called Aethiops, but these were reported to be Saracens rather than Christians. Instead of being able to report the existence of any great Christian kingdoms in the East, upon which Europe could depend for help in its Holy War against the infidels, Carpini warned his fellow Christians that the great hordes of peoples whom he had seen in his travels were in truth heathen barbarians, nations of devils bent on conquering not only the whole of Christendom but the entire world.

In 1251, or four years after Carpini's return, King Louis IX of France also dispatched to the capital of the Great Khan a mission under the leadership of a Franciscan friar named William, better known as William Rubruquis or William de Rubruck, after the name of his native town in France. Like Carpini, Friar William was also charged with making inquiries concerning the location of Prester John's empire, but the results of his mission were even more distressing than those of his predecessor. Not only did he see or hear nothing of any prince who conformed anywise to the current conception of Prester John, he brought back from the Great Khan a letter in which the Mongol potentate issued what was nothing short of an insulting ultimatum to "the most Christian king" Louis IX. The letter read in part as follows:

> This . . . is the message of the Mangu [Great] Khan to the Lord of the French. Wherever ears can hear, wherever horses can travel, there let it be heard and known, that those who do not believe, but resist our commandments, shall not be able to see with their eyes or hold with their hands or walk with their feet. . . . If you will obey us, send your ambassadors, that we may know whether you wish for peace or war. But if you say, our country is far, our mountains are strong and our sea is wide, then you will find what we can do. . . .

It is obvious that these reports, (edited by W. W. Rockhill, and published by the Hakluyt Society, London, 1900), did little to strengthen the views of those who were disposed to think that Asia was the seat of Prester John's empire. About a generation or so later, Marco Polo, on his return from a long sojourn in various parts of Asia, brought back to Europe a report about a Mongol potentate named Unc Kahn who had lived about a century before and who was identified as the "great prince—Prester John—of whom the whole world talks." This king, however, had been killed, Marco Polo reported, in a great battle with the Great Khan, and though his descendants continued to bear the title Prester John, they were not independent princes, but vassals of the Tartars. The prince who bore the title in Marco Polo's time was named George, and though he himself and some of his nobles were Christians, the majority of his subjects were pagans and Muslims. In his provinces precious stones were plentiful and of good quality, and there was "a certain amount of industry and trade," although most of the people lived by breeding camels and cattle and by reaping the "fruits of the soil."

Marco Polo's observations were therefore rather a disappointment to the peoples of Europe who were disposed to place Prester John's empire in Asia, for the picture presented by the great traveler was at odds with the traditional conceptions of the size and wealth of Prester John's domains and the incomparable magnitude of his military power. About a generation after Marco Polo's return to Europe, Friar Oderic of Pordenone, who had spent many years as a traveler and missionary in central and eastern Asia, wrote an account of his travels in which he declared that in the course of his homeward journey he had passed through what was supposed to be the Asian dominions of Prester John; but of this prince and his domains Friar Oderic reports that not "one-hundredth part" of what had been said of him and his land was true.

Thus, at the very time that the reports by Carpini, William Rubruquis, Marco Polo, and Friar Oderic were having the effect of undermining popular faith in the existence of a great Asian prince who matched in any way the traditional conceptions of Prester John, several popes were sending letters and missions to the kings of Ethiopia and some, at least, of the latter were replying in kind. That the fame of these kings and their kingdoms was not only widely current in Europe but had penetrated also deep into Asia is indicated by the fact that Marco Polo, who never reached within a thousand miles of Ethiopia, heard and recorded many interesting details about it. In the same report containing his deflating account of the Asian Prester John, Marco Polo mentioned a great African empire situated in what he called Middle India and to which he gave the name Abash. This was of course the Ethiopian region which was known to the Arab authors as Habash. Abash, according to Marco Polo, was divided into six principalities, three of which were presided over by Muslim princes and three by Christian kings, but each of these was a vassal of the Great Lord of Abash who was "a follower of the religion of Jesus Christ."

In the principalities of Abash there were "many horsemen and excellent warriors" who were "the best soldiers in this part of the world." Marco Polo then told at some length a story of how the Supreme Lord of Abash sent a mission, headed by a distinguished bishop of the realm, to Jerusalem to adorn the tomb of Christ in his name. Although the incomparable Italian traveler had chosen to identify Prester John with a third-rate Asian prince, there is little doubt that the African potentate whom he described was the real Prester John.

From Friar Oderic's time onward, few European travelers in the east, or others who felt called upon to express an opinion on the matter, ventured to make any part of Asia the seat of Prester John's empire. From then on the dominions of the celebrated priest-king were almost always identified with kingdoms or empires situated in some part of Africa. Usually they were identified with those regions which are now generally designated as Abyssinia or Ethiopia, though occasionally there were writers who placed them in other parts of the continent.

About the year 1316 William Adam, an enterprising Dominican missionary in the east, had proposed that the Christian powers of Europe, working in collaboration with Ethiopia, establish a blockade which would exclude Muslim merchants from the ports of the Red Sea; and to this end he made repeated but unsuccessful attempts to visit the African kingdom for the purpose of laying this matter before the Ethiopian king. When Adam failed to get action on this proposal, Friar Jordanus wrote a letter to Pope John XXII, urging him to join with Prester John in promoting the ambitious undertaking. No practical attempt was made, it would seem, to carry out this proposal at this particular period, but about a century later, Alphonso V of Aragon and the king of Ethiopia did make a joint effort to put a similar scheme in effect.

In a letter to certain members of his Order, Friar Jordanus urged that some of them make their way to Ethiopia and become preachers in that very populous land. In the same letter he stated that "I pray the Lord that I shall not die until I myself have been a pilgrim for the faith in that country, for that is my whole heart's desire." It would appear, however, that he was never able to realize his desire; but by identifying Ethiopia as the empire of Prester John, he rendered the country perhaps an even greater service by assuring it the renown and good will which centuries of tradition had been wont to bestow upon that mysterious land. To be sure, what he said about the great wealth and power of its potentates was based upon what he heard from others rather than what he saw with his own eyes; and it may be true that what he reported in this respect was an overstatement of the facts. However, this does not alter the fact that the report provides some clear indications of what Jordanus' informants thought about the wealth and power of Ethiopia at that time.

Most of the European travelers who followed Jordanus in the east also identified the king of Ethiopia as the widely heralded Prester John. About the year 1338, John Marignolli of Florence, a Franciscan friar, was sent by Pope Benedict XII (1334–1342) as papal legate to the East, and sometime after his return in about 1353, he wrote an account of his travels in which he specifically stated that "Aethiopia where the Negroes dwell" is the "Land of Prester John." He, too, reported that the sultan of Egypt paid Prester John tribute in order that he would not "shut off the waters of the Nile, which, should he do, would cause Egypt to perish." About the same time an anonymous Franciscan monk, who claimed that he had traveled widely in Africa, including Ethiopia, published an extended account of his wanderings. In his work he stated that the king of Ethiopia, whose name means "Servant of the Cross," was the defender of Prester John, whom he identified as the "Patriarch of Nubia and Abyssinia" and the "lord of many great lands and many cities of Christians." He stated further that the inhabitants of Prester John's domains were "Negroes as to their skins," and men of intelligence and good brains with "understanding and knowledge." Although this author makes a distinction between Prester John and the Ethiopian king, he nevertheless clearly places the king's dominions in Ethiopia.

William of Boldensel, a German nobleman of the Dominican Order, who traveled in Egypt, Palestine, and Syria in the years 1332–1333, mentioned in a published account of his wanderings that he saw in Jerusalem "Indians who held the faith of Prester John." The geographical locality of these Indians is not indicated, but as Ethiopia was frequently designated by Marco Polo and others as India or Middle India at this period, there is but little doubt that Boldensel's Indians who "held the faith of Prester John" were Ethiopians. About a generation later (circa 1350) Ludolph von Suchem, another German pilgrim-traveler, stated in his report on his sojourn in Syria and Palestine that "I know of bishops and lords who are ever wont to send accounts of this part of the East and all kinds of news across the Red Sea to Prester John." John of Hildesheim, yet another German traveler in the east, mentioned in his translation (or alleged translation) of the celebrated work, *The Three Blessed Kings* (published about 1370) that the chapel which the Ethiopians owned on Mount Calvary was dug out of the rock under the joint sponsorship of the Christians of Nubia and Prester John in Honor of the Magi, one of whom was Melchior, King of Nubia. The whereabouts of Prester John's kingdom is not specifically mentioned, but his association with the king of Nubia indicates that the author of the text evidently considered Prester John to be an African prince.

The Italian Simon Sigoli, who traveled in Egypt, Palestine, and Syria in 1384, referred to Prester John in such a way as to leave no doubt that he regarded him as an African king. For although he calls him a potentate of India, he says that he was a "neighbor of the sultan of Egypt" and the commander of the headwaters of the Nile. Had he wished, Prester John, so Sigoli reported, could have "drowned the whole of Egypt" by opening certain sluices in that part of the great river which was in his country. To induce him to refrain from doing this, the Egyptian sultan sent to Prester John every year a ball of gold, with a cross upon it, worth three thousand bezants.

Towards the end of the fourteenth century, a Franciscan monk announced that he had lived for many years in Ethiopia, which he said was the land of Prester John. The circumstances under which he had reached the country are not clear; it is possible, however, that he was one of the monks known to have labored in Ethiopia during the first half of the fourteenth century. If so, he would appear to have been one of the very few who ever returned to Europe. At any rate, his story attracted considerable attention in Spain. On one occasion he related his adventures in the presence of Count (later Cardinal) de Foix who was so much impressed by this account of Prester John and his empire that he resolved to have the king hear the whole story. Through the intercession of the count the monk was accordingly presented to His Majesty John I of Aragon on April 8, 1391. This eye-witness account had the effect of removing practically all doubt that Ethiopia was the realm of the real Prester John.

Early in the next century, direct relationships between Ethiopia and Europe became very close. On July 16, 1402, an Ethiopian embassy, under the guidance of Antonio Bartoli of Florence, arrived in Venice from the Ethiopian King Newaya Krestos. The exact destination of the ambassadors is not clear, but it is reported that they had with them spices and a leopard which were no doubt intended as gifts for the pope or the European prince to whom they had been sent. In 1408 Ethiopian pilgrims from Jerusalem are reported to have visited Bologna, Padua, and Rome. A few years after this, ambassadors from the Ethiopian King Yeshak or Isaac I (1414–1427) sent letters to the "Kings of the Franks," to the sovereign of Aragon and France, urging them to join him in an alliance against the Muslim infidels. The king of Ethiopia suggested that if they would arrange to have a fleet built in the Red Sea, he would shoulder all the expenses connected with the undertaking. The Ethiopian ambassadors were received by the king of Aragon at Valencia in the presence of Cardinal de Foix, the papal legate who later reported the matter to Pope Martin V.

The ambassadors informed the king that their sovereign reigned over sixty-two princes, twelve of whom were Muslims and the others Christians. Alphonso and Charles readily agreed to the Ethiopian king's proposals and took active steps to cement the alliance. The king of Aragon even proposed strengthening the alliance through a double marriage between members of his house and the royal family of Ethiopia. It was suggested that his daughter, the Infanta Dona Juana, marry the king of Ethiopia, and that Alphonso's son, the Infant Don Pedro, wed some suitable Ethiopian princess. These proposals were sent to the Ethiopian king in a letter which bore the salutation: "Isaac, son of David, by the Grace of God, master of the Indies, possessor of the Tablets of Sinai and the Throne of David, Prester John, King of Kings of Ethiopia." The letter was entrusted for delivery to the Aragonese king's own chaplain who was assisted on his way by the grand master of Rhodes and the king of Cyprus. The chaplain reportedly was well versed in Arabic, and on leaving Rhodes went to Jerusalem and from there departed secretly by way of Egypt for Ethiopia. What happened after that is not clear, but it would appear that the union of the two houses was ultimately consummated in accordance with the king of Aragon's plan.*

The king of France responded to Prester John's proposal for an alliance by sending a mission to Ethiopia to negotiate with the Ethiopian king on the matter. The mission, composed of a Frenchman, a Spaniard, and a native of Naples, went to Alexandria from which its members set out for Ethiopia by way of Egypt and the Red Sea. Two of the

---

* Alphonso revived the political aspects of the scheme in 1450.

emissaries, the Frenchman and the Spaniard, died; however, in the course of the journey, Pietro, the Neapolitan, seems eventually to have reached the Ethiopian capital. He was seen a few years later—about 1432—in Constantinople where he was busy recruiting shipbuilders for the Ethiopians, a fact which seems to indicate that he had carried the first part of his mission to a successful conclusion. Whether or not the ships were ever actually built in the Red Sea is not known, but it is certain that the purpose for which they were intended—a united Ethiopian, French, and Aragonese attack by sea on Egypt—was never realized. One reason for the failure of the proposed scheme was that Jacques Couers, the finance minister of Charles VII, was eager to revive French trade in the eastern Mediterranean basin, and to do this he thought it better to have the good will rather than the enmity of the Muslim sultan of Egypt. But these missions and negotiations did have the effect of removing whatever doubt may still have lingered in the minds of European princes concerning the whereabouts of Prester John's empire.

According to a letter of Pope Eugenius IV dated August 9, 1431, an Ethiopian embassy, headed by one Brother Thomas, is said to have arrived in Rome where it was royally received as was befitting the emissaries of the great Prester John. Tradition reports that the pope granted forty days of grace to all who contributed toward making their stay in the Eternal City a pleasant one. After having prayed at the tombs of the Apostles Peter and Paul, the emissaries returned to Jerusalem and Ethiopia.

About ten years later another Ethiopian delegation arrived in Italy to participate in the deliberations of the historic Ecumenical Council of Florence. Nothing perhaps indicates more clearly the exalted position which Prester John had come to occupy in the thought of the day than does the extent to which the pope went to insure the presence of Ethiopian representation at that celebrated gathering. The same attitude of high regard for the African kingdom is also reflected in the enthusiastic welcome which was accorded the Ethiopian delegates to the Council, for the representatives of no other nation were more warmly greeted by the pope and the other princes of the Church.

The Council was convened by Pope Eugenius IV (1431–1447) with the hope of finding some way to bring various churches of the east (the Greek Catholic, the Jacobite, the Armenian Nestorian) into union with the Roman Catholic Church. One of the principal purposes of this proposed union was to rally the whole of Christendom behind the pope's ambitious plan for a concerted Christian campaign against the Muslims of the East, who were then rising to new and unprecedented power under the leadership of the Ottoman Turks. Eugenius, like many European Christians of that age, had been profoundly impressed by the long-standing reports of the military prowess of Prester John's empire. Now that it had been definitely determined that Ethiopia and the domain of the great priest-king were one and the same, the pope was exceptionally eager that the Ethiopians should become active participants in the efforts for a united confederation of Christian peoples. To this end, a distinguished Franciscan friar, Alberto da Sarteano, was dispatched by Pope Eugenius IV as his legate to the Levant with letters to the various Christian princes and patriarchs of the east, inviting them to send delegates to an ecumenical council which was scheduled to open in Ferrara in 1438.

Among these letters was one to John XI, the patriarch of the Coptic Church in Egypt, and another to Prester John, king of the Ethiopians. The Coptic patriarch was not very enthusiastic about the union but he did agree to send delegates to the council. Thus, while in Egypt, Albert da Sarteano is said to have asked the sultan to grant him the right to travel through his country to Ethiopia, for he was eager to present in person the pope's invitation to Prester John, but the sultan denied the request.

It appears that sometime before his stop in Egypt, the

papal legate had already visited Jerusalem where he had discussed at length the objectives of the council with Abbot Nicodemus, the head of the Ethiopian monastery in the holy city. Although the head of the establishment had certain plenipotentiary powers and had long been an intermediary through which negotiations were carried on between the Ethiopians and the Holy See, the abbot did not have the power to commit his government to any major change in public policy without prior instructions from or subsequent approval by the king.

Ever since the establishment of Christianity in the country in the fourth century, the Ethiopian Christians had regarded themselves as members of the Jacobite or Coptic Church and had acknowledged the patriarch of Alexander, rather than the Roman Catholic pope, as their supreme spiritual leader. It is true that certain Ethiopian kings in the past appear to have considered the idea of transferring their allegiance to the Roman Catholic Church, but no definite actions had been taken in that direction. Since one of the major objectives of the Ferrara council called by Pope Eugenius, was to find ways and means of establishing a definite union between the Roman and the Ethiopian Church, Abbot Nicodemus, aware no doubt of the sympathetic attitude of the earlier kings towards this matter, had every reason to suppose that his government would look with favor upon the suggested union. When, therefore, the matter was presented to him by the papal ambassador, the abbot readily agreed to cooperate in the effort. On his own authority he promptly appointed a delegation of Ethiopian monks to attend the council as representatives of his country and his king, and he instructed them to participate actively in the council's deliberations. He made it clear, however, to his appointees, and to the papal ambassador that the former had no authority to make any final commitments on the proposed union and that none of their concessions and decisions in this respect could be considered as binding agreements until they had been reviewed and approved by the king.

Although Alberto da Sarteano had to accept this arrangement, he appears not to have been satisfied with it. He seems to have thought that if he could talk with Prester John himself, some way would be found through which speedier and more definitive action could be taken on the matter. With this in mind, the papal ambassador and a small group of companions are said to have departed Jerusalem to reach Ethiopia by way of Mesopotamia, the Persian Gulf, and the Indian Ocean. In the course of this journey, however, the ambassador fell ill and was forced to abandon the effort, but he urged his companions to proceed and to do their best to bring it to a successful conclusion. This they endeavored to do but were subsequently captured by pirates and held in captivity for several years. They were eventually liberated through the efforts of the papal ambassador who was provided with funds for their ransom by the treasury of the Holy See.

In 1441, the Ethiopian delegation to the council set out from Jerusalem for Florence, for the council had been transferred from Ferrara to Florence. The delegation included twelve Ethiopian monks and their guide, an Italian merchant from Sienna. At the head of the delegation was Peter the Deacon, who later acquitted himself well on the council floor as the chief spokesman of his group and church. On the island of Rhodes, the Ethiopians were joined by the papal ambassador himself who henceforward served as their chief escort. News that the Ethiopians were on their way reached Italy some weeks before the delegation arrived.

Prior to the receipt of news of the Ethiopians' arrival, two of the major objectives of the council had already been achieved. After considerable debate and negotiations the delegates representing the Greek Catholic Church had voted to accept the proposed union with the Roman Catholic Church, and a concordat to this effect had been signed on July 5, 1439. The delegates representing the Armenian

Church had signed a similar agreement on November twenty-second of the same year. In each of these agreements the pope of Rome had been acknowledged as the supreme head of the Christian Church. Thus, when the news arrived that the Ethiopian delegates were on their way, it was assumed that they too were coming for the purpose of signing an agreement to the same effect; for it appears that the papal legate had not disclosed to the pope that Peter the Deacon and his colleagues did not have plenipotentiary power in this matter. In addition to the pope's strong wishes that the Ethiopians should pledge themselves to the union so that he would have their support in the grand campaign he was planning against the Muslim Turks, there was another reason for his eagerness to have their cooperation. In 1439 the enemies of Eugenius IV, meeting in a "rump convention" at Basel, had voted to dispose of the Holy Father and had elected the Duke of Savoy, Felix V (known as the anti-pope) in his place. Although the church as a whole had maintained its allegiance to Eugenius IV, he was aware that the anti-pope movement could not be ignored and might indeed become dangerous if steps were not taken to counteract its growth and influence. He realized that the signing of the concordats with the Greeks and the Armenians had done much to increase his prestige and offset the effects of the anti-papal movement. But signing a similar agreement with Prester John, who in prestige and renown was surpassed by no Christian prince, would further boost the pope's prestige. We may well believe, therefore, that the old medieval chronicler wrote the truth when he reported that the pope was quite beside himself with joy when he learned that the Ethiopian embassy was on its way to Italy. When this news arrived the pope promptly recommended that the council should be moved at once to Rome in order that the "splendid embassy" which was being sent to Italy by the "High and Mighty Emperor of Ethiopia" for the purpose of "submitting his Church and his Empire to the Pope" should not find the Council sitting in such a paltry town as Florence, but in the eternal city itself, the great "metropolis of the Christian world."

According to one account, the pope's recommendation was favorably received and the council was transferred to Rome. This account may be true, for it is known that later meetings of the council did indeed take place in the Lateran Palace at Rome; but according to some authorities the removal of the council from Florence did not occur until 1443. If this date is correct, the council still must have been in session in Florence when the Ethiopian delegates arrived, for it is generally supposed that they reached Italy in the summer or fall of 1441. What is certain, however, is that the pope and the members of the council received the Ethiopian delegation with open arms and accorded it every honor at their command. And there does not seem to have been any difference in the warmth of the reception even after the limited authority of the Ethiopian delegates was revealed. There is little doubt that this was due to the skillful diplomacy displayed by the Ethiopians in this delicate situation.

Abbot Nicodemus, with more astuteness than his biblical namesake, had sent to the pope an adroitly worded letter in which he assured the Holy Father that he was quite sure that when his king learned of the proposed union of the churches, it should bring "the greatest pleasure" to him, for he "has always been eager to see all Christendom united into one great common faith." This statement may have been deliberately sibylline in character, for it could well have meant that the Ethiopian king was eager to see all Christendom united under the Jacobite or Ethiopic rather than the Roman Catholic Church. At any rate, the pope seems to have read no such meaning into it; for he appears to have been much gratified by the letter and its contents. The pope seems to have been equally pleased with what Peter the Deacon and his comrades said of the proposed union in their discourses before the council, and perhaps in their private conversations as well.

Fortunately, the text of at least one of the speeches made by Peter The Deacon on the floor of the council has been preserved. From this we learn that while he did not, as he could not, make any definite pledge that the Ethiopians would accept the union on the same terms as had the Armenians and the Greeks, the text of the speech does indicate that he and his comrades were deeply sympathetic towards a union of some kind and labored honestly and faithfully to work out an agreement that would be satisfactory both to the pope and to their country, church, and king.

The head of the Ethiopian delegation made no attempt to obscure the doctrinal differences which had long characterized the tenets of his own and those of the Roman Catholic faith. He called attention especially to the Ethiopian and the Roman Catholic points of view concerning the nature of Christ and the Procession of the Holy Ghost. In his disputations with the papal theologians he defended with learning, logic, and vigor the position taken by his Church on these grave questions; but his arguments presented no barriers which the conferees were not able to surmount. For it is apparent from the annals of the time that despite the doctrinal differences mentioned, the Ethiopians and the papal representatives arrived at an agreement respecting the proposed union that was satisfactory to both groups. To be sure, this agreement required the approval by the Ethiopian king before its provisions could become effective. Notwithstanding its conditional character, however, the pope appears to have accepted the agreement with good grace and was hopeful enough about its ultimate prospects. He signified his gratitude toward the Ethiopian delegates for the part they had played in the negotiations by taking special steps to insure that the remainder of their stay in Italy would be as pleasant as he could make it. He supplied them with a letter of introduction in which they were commended to all as worthy ambassadors of the great King Prester John and provided them with a special permit which enabled them to inspect the sacred and closely guarded relics associated with the Passion of Christ and the lives of the saints, which then, as now, constitute the most venerated treasures of the Roman Catholic Church. It is specially mentioned that during their visit to St. Peter's cathedral the Ethiopians were shown the *vera icon* or the veil which pious tradition alleged had been employed by Saint Veronica to wipe the sweat from the brow of Jesus when he was bending under the Cross while on his way to Calvary.

For centuries a painting that portrayed the members of this Ethiopian mission was preserved at the Vatican, and it is not unlikely that this was executed at the special request of the pope. Two hundred years later a celebrated Ethiopian monk, while on a visit to Rome, was shown this painting, and though he knew nothing of their mission, he recognized the men in the picture as his compatriots from the character of their dress. Some scholars have suggested that it was probably during the visit of this mission to Italy that the Ethiopians were granted the right to establish the monastery which they maintained in Rome for many generations. Others have supposed that this establishment dates back to a much earlier period, while yet others think it was not founded until the time of Pope Sixtus IV (1471–1484).[*]

[*] There can be no doubt about the great power and prestige of Ethiopia in international relations during the early modern era. The Christian faith reinforced the monarchy and both became symbols and bonds of identity and unity for Ethiopians, and this was further buttressed by the international image of the country. Not only did Europe and Asia identify Prester John's kingdom as Ethiopia, the kings and their emissaries identified themselves and their constituents internationally as Ethiopians. Thus, the monarchy, the church, and the impact of international relations combined to establish an indelible sense of identity which manifested itself in the continuity of general unity and of independence for Ethiopia throughout the era of colonialism in Africa, except for the Italian invasion and occupation (1936–40), to the present day.

Bibliography

There is no way to list all the sources Professor Hansberry examined in the course of his research for these essays. He studied in the field of African history, with a special focus on Ethiopia, for nearly fifty years and thus was well qualified to formulate his own conclusions. No doubt many works in the field of anthropology, archaeology, history, art, contributed to his final assessments, but only he could have prepared a definitive list of those works. What follows, therefore, is a list compiled on the basis of those sources which appeared in connection with these essays and lectures he gave on the subjects.

Profile of a Pioneer Africanist

This chapter is based primarily on William Leo Hansberry's private papers which are in the possession of his wife, Myrtle Kelso Hansberry.

Eulogies following Hansberry's death include: Nnamdi Azikiwe, "Eulogy on William Leo Hansberry," *Negro History Bulletin*, XXVIII, (December, 1965); Williston H. Lofton, "William Leo Hansberry: The Man and His Mission," *Freedomways*, vol. VI, no. 2, Second Quarter (1966); Raymond J. Smyke, "William Leo Hansberry: Tribute to a Heretic," *Africa Report* (November, 1965), and "Pioneer Africanist," *West Africa* (November 20, 1965).

More recent and substantive articles on Hansberry are: James Spady, "Dr. William Leo Hansberry: The Legacy of an

152 *Bibliography*

African Hunter," *A Current Bibliography on African Affairs,*
vol. 3, no. 10 (November-December, 1970); "A Tribute to the
Memory of Professor William Leo Hansberry," Howard University History Department, November 20, 1972; "William Leo
Hansberry and Ancient African History," *Department of History, Howard University,* 1913-1973, pp. 43-54.

Chapter I

Al-Tabari, Muhammad Ibn Jarir, *Annals* (ed., M. J. de Goeje,
London, 1902).

Budge, E. A. Wallis, *The Queen of Sheba and Her Only Son
Menyelek* (London, 1922).

Le Roux, H., *Chez la Reine de Saba: Chronique Ethiopienne*

Stern, Henry A., *Wanderings Among the Falashas* (London,
1862).

Telles, Balthazar, *Historia geral da Ethiopia a Alta* (n.p., 1660).

———, *Extrait de l'histoire d'Ethiopie écrite en Portugais* (n.p.,
1674).

———, *The Travels of the Jesuits in Ethiopia* (n.p., 1710), a
translation.

Weil, Gustav, *Biblische Legenden der Muselmanner* (Frankfurt,
1845).

Chapters II & III

Baronius, Caesar, *Annales Ecclesiastici* (Rome, 1588-1607).

Budge, E. A. Wallis, *The Book of the Bee* (London, 1886).

———, *The Book of the Saints of the Ethiopian Church* (London, 1928).

Charles, R. H., *Chronicle of John, Bishop of Nikiu* (n.p., 1916).

Crichton, Andrew, *History of Arabia* (Edinburgh, 1833).

Geddes, Michael, *The Church History of Ethiopia* (London,
1696).

Josephus, Flavius, *Histoire des Juifs* (Paris, 1667).

Latourette, K. S., *A History of the Expansion of Christianity*
(London, 1939).

Michel, Francisque and Thomas Wright, *Relation des Voyages
de Guillaume de Rubruk* (Paris, 1839).

Moberg, A., *The Book of the Himyarites* (London & Paris, 1924).

Rockhill, W. W., *The Journey of William of Rubruck* (London, 1900).

Salih, Muhammad, *Deze Ketab es can Salaah op de Madhab* . . . (Kaaptad, 1906).

Tyrannius, Rufinus, Historia Ecclesiasticae (n.p., 1535).

Vasilev, Aleksandr A., *Justin the First* (Cambridge, Mass., 1950).

Wright, Thomas, *Early Christianity in Arabia* (London, 1855).

Yule, Henry, Jordanus [Catalani] (London, 1863)

Chapter IV

Beazley, C. Ramond, *Dawn of Modern Geography* (London, 1897-1906), 3 vols.

Bruce, James, *Travels Through Abyssinia* (Edinburgh, 1807); *Travels to Discover the Source of the Nile* (London, 1790).

Budge, E. A. Wallis, *History of Ethiopia, Nubia, and Abyssinia* (London, 1928).

———, "Annals of Nubian Kings," *Egyptian Literature* (London, 1912), II.

———, *The Egyptian Sudan* (London, 1907).

Cary, M. and E. H. Warmington, *The Ancient Explorers* (London, 1929).

Coquebert-Montbret, M., *Recueil de Voyages et de Memoirs* (Paris, 1839).

de la Ronciere, Charles Bourel, *La Découverte de l'Afrique au Moyen Age* (Cairo, 1924).

———, *La Geographie de l'Egypte à Travers les Ages* (Paris, 1931).

Doresse, Jeane, L'Empire du Prêtre-Jean (Paris, 1957).

———, *Ethiopia* (trans., London and New York, 1959).

Kammerer, Albert, *La Mer Rouge, l'Abyssinie depuis l'Antiquité* (Cairo, 1929, 1935, 1947), vols. 1-3.

Ludolf, Hiob (Jobus Ludolphus), *Historia Ethiopica* (Frankfurt, 1681).

Morie, Louis J., *Histoire de L'Ethiopie* (Paris, 1904).

Oppert, Gustav, *Der Presbyter Johannes in Sage und Geschichte* (Berlin, 1964).

Ross, E. Denison, "Prester John and the Empire of Ethiopia," in *Travel and Travellers in the Middle Ages* (New York, 1926, ed., A. P. Newton).

Theal, G. M., *Records of South-Eastern Africa* (London, 1898).

Wright, Thomas, *The Travels of Marco Polo* (London, 1854).

Yule, Henry, *The Book of Ser Marco Polo* (London, 1903).

Zarncke, Frederick, "Der Priester Johannes," *Abhandlungen* (Saxon Academy, 1879 and 1883), vols. VII, VIII.